Children and Decision Making

Children and Decision Making

Ian Butler, Margaret Robinson and Lesley Scanlan

Joseph Rowntree Foundation

The Joseph Rowntree Foundation has supported this project as part of its programme of research and innovative development projects, which it hopes will be of value to policy-makers, practitioners and service users.

National Children's Bureau

NCB promotes the voices, interests and well-being of all children and young people across every aspect of their lives. As an umbrella body for the children's sector in England and Northern Ireland, we provide essential information on policy, research and best practice for our members and other partners.

NCB aims to:

- challenge disadvantage in childhood
- work with children and young people to ensure they are involved in all matters that affect their lives
- promote multidisciplinary cross-agency partnership and good practice
- influence government through policy development and advocacy
- undertake high quality research and work from an evidence-based perspective
- disseminate information to all those working with children and young people, and to children and young people themselves.

The views expressed in this book are those of the authors and not necessarily those of the National Children's Bureau, the Joseph Rowntree Foundation or University of Cardiff.

Published by the National Children's Bureau for the Joseph Rowntree Foundation

National Children's Bureau, 8 Wakley Street, London EC1V 7QE
Tel: 020 7843 6000.
Website: www.ncb.org.uk
Registered Charity number 258825

© Research and Consultancy Division, University of Cardiff 2005

Published 2005

ISBN 1 904787 54 1

British Library Cataloguing in Publication Data
A catalogue record for this book is available from the British Library

Contents

Acknowledgements

The researchers would like to thank the children and young people who helped us for the pleasure of meeting them and of hearing what they had to say on the subject of decision making in families. We hope that we have accurately reflected your views and opinions in this report. We would also like to thank the headteachers and staff of the schools that provided us with the opportunity of talking to you.

We also very much want to acknowledge the advice, active support and constructive criticism provided by the project's advisory group:

Dorit Brown, Chief Executive, Parentline Plus
Professor Adrian James, Sheffield University
Dr. Nick Lee, Keele University
Charles Prest, Head of Legal Services, CAFCASS
Caroline Thomas, Senior Research Fellow, Stirling University
Anne Crowley, Policy Advisor, Save the Children
Peter Clarke, Children's Commissioner for Wales

We are particularly grateful also to Susan Taylor, Principal Research Manager of the Joseph Rowntree Foundation, for her role in coordinating and managing the project and for ensuring that the researchers' relationship with the funder has been so positive and, we think, so productive.

Ian Butler

Margaret Robinson

Lesley Scanlan

January 2005

1. Introduction

1.1 Conceptual origins of the project

This study was established 'to investigate, with children, how they negotiate their involvement in family functioning, rule-making and day-to-day domestic decision making'. Our interest in the degree to which children 'participate' in family life can be seen as part of a developing interest in the social construction of childhood and the lived experiences of children that has developed among researchers, policy-makers and a growing range of 'childcare' professionals over the last 25 years. (See, for example, James and Prout 1991; Quartrup 1994; James and James 2004.)

Central to recent sociological, political and professional interest in the structures and processes of childhood has been the degree to which children might be understood as significant authors of their own biographies. An increasing number of professional and policy discourses affecting children are infused these days with a rhetoric of 'participation' and 'partnership'. Drawing on 'rights-speak' and the steady consumerisation of public services, for example, children, in the opening years of the 21st century, seem likely to be drawn into negotiated arrangements with their social workers or their teachers to an extent that would have been almost unimaginable even half a generation ago. We make no comment here on how much progress from 'marginality to citizenship' (Wintersberger 1996) has actually been achieved by children over recent years as this is beyond the scope of this report.

We do incline to the view however that, in so far as children make or are involved in decisions about the conduct of their own lives, they do so largely in those areas defined for them by adults and on adults' terms (see Alanen 1994; Neale 2002). Historically, research has reflected this in the way that it has focused largely on the experience of 'clinical' populations of children: that is to say, children identified as troubled or troublesome.

The programme of research reported here is heir to this 'tradition' in so far as it is an account of an aspect of their lives provided by children at the request of adults, but it differs in two key respects. First, the children whose views, experiences and opinions we report here are 'ordinary' children, drawn from ordinary communities in south east Wales (for further details see Section 1.3 and Appendix 1). They are not, in the main, subject to any particular interest by the state nor are they, generally speaking, undergoing any particular stress or negotiating any problematic transition. Second, the subject of our inquiries is the everyday. It is the means, processes, habits of thought, customs and rituals through which children and their parents negotiate the routine business of domestic life. We do not explore children's relationships with the agencies of the local or national state, nor any of their informal relationships beyond the domestic hearth. Indeed, one of our primary interests in conducting this research was to establish, for the first time, reliable 'baseline' data for better understanding children's experience of decision making prior to their engagement with more structured forms of participation, especially in formal or 'clinical' settings.

Our interest in family life and the role played by children in the subtle, complex and dynamic processes of everyday domestic decision making arose out of our previous work on children's experience of their parents' divorce (Butler and others 2003; Robinson and others 2003 and forthcoming). We noted there the active role played by children in the management of their own and their parents' lives during and immediately after the crisis of parental separation. This provided us with a glimpse of what Giddens has called the 'democratisation of the private sphere' (1992: 184). This process of transition from 'hierarchical' to 'democratic' forms of intergenerational relationships represents a fundamental and historically significant change in the nature of the family. It is one in which the participants in any intimate relationship 'determine and regulate the conditions of their association' (1992: 185). By exploring children's participation in family decision making, using children as our 'unit of observation and as mediators of information' (Quartrup 1994: 6), we hoped that we might contribute indirectly to understanding how far this 'democratisation' actually extends to children.

More importantly, we hope that our research contributes to our developing understanding of children as significant contributors to their own 'biographical projects' (Buchner and others 1995), as social 'actors' in their own domestic lives. In this way, we hope to provide a basis from which to identify the means whereby their participation might be nurtured, developed and extended into other forms and settings.

1.2 The structure of the report

The remainder of this chapter describes how we gathered our data. The following three chapters present our findings: Chapter 2 describes some of the central dynamics of family decision making and the application of family rules, and raises issues concerning the authority of parents and the differentiated roles that mothers and fathers play in family decision making; Chapters 3 and 4 explore some variations on these patterns and, in particular, report data describing children's progress towards more autonomy in decision making. Chapter 5 explores in detail the idea of 'fairness' and its importance to children. The final chapter attempts to synthesise these findings and offers some reflections on their possible implications.

1.3 Research method and process

Our study was designed as a two-stage process. In Phase 1, we set out to 'map the territory' of family decision making, using group-based forms of data collection. In Phase 2, using a blend of semi-structured interviews and a number of workbook 'activities' to collect both qualitative and quantitative data, we examined in greater depth the salient issues arising from Phase 1. (See Butler and others 2003: 14 ff. for a more detailed discussion of our general approach to combining qualitative and quantitative methodologies.) A more detailed account of the research methods used in this study is given in Appendix 1.

1.3.1 Building the sample

The children who took part in our study were recruited via their primary schools and were all in the age range 8–11 years. The schools involved were chosen at random from four local education authority (LEA) areas in south Wales covering a cross section of city, rural and urban communities. The urban communities included examples of a post-industrial (ex-mining) community and a new town community. A total of eight schools participated. All the fieldwork for the study was conducted on school premises and in school time. In each school the help of teachers was sought to ensure that the children who participated comprised a cross section of the school's population, particularly in terms of age, gender, academic ability and ethnicity.

1.3.2 Phase 1: Participants

Sixty-nine children, from four schools, took part in Phase 1. The sample comprised:

- Urban school (post-industrial): 11 girls and nine boys, average age 9.5 years.
- Urban school (new town): seven girls and eight boys, average age 9.8 years.
- City school: nine girls and seven boys, average age 9.0 years. Five children were from ethnic minority families.
- Rural school: seven girls and 11 boys, average age 9.3 years.

1.3.3 Phase 1: Data collection and analysis

A 'quick-think' task and set of family decision vignettes were designed for the study and used to stimulate discussion with small groups of children on everyday family decision making. Two group sessions were conducted in each school and groups comprised seven to ten children. Children also provided demographic data by means of an 'About me' exercise. The researchers worked in pairs to facilitate the group sessions.

The quick-think task generated a list of specific decisions within the experience of each group, and stimulated general discussion on decisions in which children were or were not involved. The vignettes stimulated open, wide-ranging discussion, including spontaneous accounts of children's own experience of decision making. The analysis indicated that across the eight groups, children raised a number of common decision-making points, characterised (on presentation) by the topic or substance of the decision in question:

- clothes and appearance
- children's free time, particularly spending time with or going out with friends (covering issues of child safety and parental concern, such as 'stranger danger')
- family routines, including bedtimes and mealtimes
- family activities, including outings, holidays, watching TV, special events (such as Christmas, birthdays)
- 'big' family decisions, including moving or buying a new house, home improvements (such as decorating), large purchases (a car, TV, computer and so on).

As well as identifying some of the common topics of decision making, the analysis suggested a number of common themes that cut across the various topics of domestic decision making:

- competence and autonomy of children
- authority and competence of adults
- nature and scope of children's involvement in family decision making
- fairness.

Both the 'topic' and thematic data were used to inform the development of the data collection instruments for Phase 2 of the study.

1.3.4 Phase 2: Participants

As the direction of data collection in Phase 2 was driven by findings from Phase 1, Phase 2 schools were matched with those in Phase 1 to increase the likelihood of participants being aware of, and able to discuss, issues highlighted by their peers in Phase 1.

Forty-eight children, from four schools, took part in Phase 2. The sample comprised:

- Urban school (post-industrial): six girls and six boys, average age 9.8 years.
- Urban school (new town): seven girls and five boys, average age 9.8 years.
- City school: 10 girls and two boys, average age 10.5 years; five children were from ethnic minority families.
- Rural school: seven girls and five boys, average age 9.7 years.

The samples for both phases were drawn from the same 'key stage' school classes. Phase 1 was conducted in February 2003 and Phase 2 in June 2003; consequently children in the second phase were slightly older than those in the first.[1]

1.3.5 Phase 2: Data collection and analysis

Children were interviewed individually using an interview schedule designed to examine more closely the topics, themes and issues highlighted by children in Phase 1. Using data derived from the quick-think task, the most frequently cited topics for decisions were chosen as the basis for interview questions. These were varied in 'scale' (measured in terms of potential consequences, from the trivial to the life changing) reflecting the Phase 1 'thematic' data.

Building also on Phase 1 data, a set of core interview questions was developed to explore each decision. The prompts were designed, broadly, to explore:

---

1   It is for this reason that the body of this report does not contain any verbatim contributions from those aged less than 9, as all the quotations used derive from Phase 2 of the data collection process.

- how the decision was made
- who was involved
- what part the child played
- whether or not the same decision or rules applied to other family members and under what circumstances
- what the child felt about the decision-making process
- what changes the child would like to make to the decision-making process and why.

As well as exploring specific topics, we asked more general questions so as to explore additional thematic strands (such as fairness) identified in Phase 1.

In addition to the interviews, children provided demographic information and completed measures assessing dimensions of family functioning,[2] child–parent communication, child involvement and self-worth (see Appendix 1). These data were collected by means of an Activity Book designed for the purpose.

The analysis of Phase 2 data forms the greater part of the remainder of this report.

1.3.6 Research confidentiality and anonymity

Prior to starting each Phase 1 group session and each Phase 2 interview, the researchers ensured that potential participants had given their consent freely and with an understanding of the nature and purpose of the study. The nature of confidentiality was explained.

To preserve anonymity in the presentation of our findings, children's names, and those of family and friends they mentioned while talking to us, are all pseudonyms with each name applied consistently. Most other non-essential details, including locations, have also been changed.

1.3.7 Recording and analysis of study data

The Phase 1 group sessions and Phase 2 interviews were recorded and the tapes transcribed verbatim. These qualitative data were content analysed with the aid of the software package Nud*Ist. The Phase 1 demographic data and Phase 2 Activity Book data were analysed using the statistical package SPSS.

---

2   These are defined as:
- Cohesion: commitment, help, support family members provide each other.
- Expressiveness: tendency to act openly and express feelings directly.
- Conflict: openly expressed anger, aggression, conflict.

2.   Making decisions

2.1 Introduction

In this chapter, we describe some of the central dynamics of family decision making and the application of family rules. We use the term 'decision' most commonly to refer to single instances where choices have to be made or questions resolved. Family 'rules' might be thought of as the 'standing decisions' of families, where, through the application of more general principles or appeals to precedent, particular matters can be settled.

Our conversations with children revealed very few examples of formal, explicit decision-making structures or processes operating within families. Indeed, the material presented in this chapter tends to suggest that, more commonly, decision making is situational and dynamic. As such, family decision making is revealed as a complex process. We consider the implications for policy and practice of this disarmingly simple observation below (Chapter 6) but it is important to recognise that it has implications too for the manner in which we present our data and for the way in which it is to be understood.

To describe family decision making as complex is to point to the fact that it cannot easily be understood without reference to all of the components of which it is comprised. This includes all of the individuals involved, their behaviours, attitudes and values, and all of the relationships that each person has with others. The sum of these various parts makes up the particular family's micro-culture in which specific decisions are made. This micro-culture also stands in some relation to the wider networks and systems in which the family is embedded. Thus family decision making has an ecological dimension in the sense that boundaries between the family and the outside world are porous.

As has been suggested (Bar-Yam 2003: 1), 'to understand the behaviour of a complex system we must understand not only the behaviour of the parts but how they act together to form the behaviour of the whole'. We recognise that we have engaged with the complexity inherent in family life from a single standpoint, that of the child and so we can make only limited claims to fully understand what we describe. More importantly, we would wish to discourage in the reader any tendency towards categorisation that does not recognise the partial view that we have taken of the processes and events that we describe. We are mindful of the tension that exists between a (social) science wishing to universalise and one that seeks to specify. Ours is essentially a descriptive exercise, albeit partial, of a specific complex system of interactions. Our decision to employ a largely qualitative methodology is consistent with this approach.

While we have sought to synthesise our data at points and to make connections between observations, we have resisted the temptation, as far as possible, to taxonomise or to simplify. Where there are inconsistencies, we have not tried to smooth them out. We have not assumed that only a few parameters are important. We have not tried to reduce what we have observed to only a few salient points. In this way, and largely using the words of the children themselves, we have tried to capture and to reflect the richness, variety and subtlety of the processes that children described to us.

2.2 Deciding family business

In this section, we pay particular attention to those areas of domestic decision making that are to do with whole-family life, as opposed to those that are concerned with individual family members, especially those concerned directly and exclusively with children (see Section 1.3.3). These more nuanced analyses are the subjects of later sections, and particularly of Chapters 3 and 4. In this section, we distinguish between two 'levels' of decision: routine (such as what to eat for tea, what to watch on TV, where to go on holiday) and one-off or life-changing ones (choice of school, moving house and so on).

Whole-family decisions by definition affect a number of people, and in relation to such decisions the children to whom we spoke described various forms of 'democracy' (see Section 1.1) in which they themselves played an active part. Children themselves do not refer to 'democracy' although the term is a useful shorthand for our purposes. They do however draw on an important, related concept, that of fairness. This is the subject of further analysis in Chapter 5.

In relation to such everyday matters as watching TV or deciding what to have for tea, children described processes involving consensual decision making, majority decision making and turn-taking:

Int.: Who makes the final decision about what you have for tea?

T: We all do.

Int.: Do you think that's a good way of doing it?

T: Yea 'cos we all get a say in it and have the food that we like.

Tom, aged 11

The children who talked about how their family decided what TV programme or video to watch similarly described processes that gave everyone a say. For example, 10-year-old Kath told us:

We would, like, pick something that we all like to watch.

Rather than the consensual approach of Kath's family to TV or Tom's family to teatime, Ellen's family opted for a simple majority in both situations:

Int.: How would you decide what you're going to watch? Who would choose?

E: Well, we don't really. We look at what's on TV and then we see something really good and mostly everyone in the room wants to watch it.

E: I just say what I really want to eat. If loads of people want that one, and I like it anyway, then I'll just have it anyway.

Ellen, aged nine

Others families, including Holly's and Zara's, opted for turn-taking.

Int.: Who decides what you'll have to eat?

H: Us – me, my brother and my sister. It's my sister on a Monday, and my brother on a Tuesday, me on a Wednesday, then it's my brother and my sister and me again. But then we're not allowed to have all different.

Int.: Does mum ever get a turn?

H: When we argue over it she just chooses things to have.

Holly, aged 11

Int.: What do you think you fancy having tonight?

Z: Fish fingers and chips.

Int.: Will your brother have fish fingers and chips if you're having it?

Z:	Yea.
Int.:	What if he doesn't want them?
Z:	He'll have to have it.
Int.:	So, he has to have what you've asked for?
Z:	Yes, but he'll get to choose the next day.

Zara, aged nine

In relation to still everyday but less frequently encountered areas of family life, such as deciding where to go on an outing or on holiday, similarly 'democratic' but possibly even more explicit and more inclusive processes were described to us. For example, most children reported having a direct say in family outings (20 out of the 24 children for whom data were available) and family holidays (30 out of 38 children).

In respect of outings, there was a fairly even divide among families between consensus and majority decision making, with a few families favouring turn-taking. Although nine-year-old Amy and her brothers (aged six and 11) who saw their dad at weekends because her parents were divorced, described a process with elements of all three.

A:	Well, we go out with dad to places like MegaBowl and go on picnics or the cinema.
Int.:	Who chooses where you go?
A:	We all decide together.
Int.:	What if all three children want something different?
A:	We decide on one and on the next week we do the other and the week after that we'd do the other.
Int.:	If you all want different things one week who finally decides which order you do them?
A:	Mmm ... well, we'll just decide and see what's best really.

In comparison to Amy's family, Natasha's family employed a strictly democratic system of voting.

Int.:	Who gets to choose where you're going to go?
N:	No one chooses really. Say mum and dad want Pizza Hut and all of us four kids want McDonald's, mum and dad will take us to McDonald's 'cos that was our vote.
Int.:	Do you think that's a good way of deciding things like that?
N:	Yea.

Natasha, aged nine

As well as describing essentially democratic and 'fair' processes, several of the preceding quotations also hint at the way in which decisions are 'cumulative' in the sense that what happens at one point may determine what happens the next time the same or a similar issue arises. The sense of decision making having a temporal dimension adds to our understanding of the complexity of the larger processes being described. It also suggests the importance of being able to draw on a stock of common experience, an intimate and minute knowledge of the past when coming to acceptable decisions in families. We return below (Section 4.5) to the importance of 'tradition' and precedent in family decision making.

Some children have already indicated that if a dispute cannot be resolved 'democratically', the final decision rests with parents (see also Section 2.3 ff.). For example, of the children who talked about teatime, 30 said their mother made the final decision, three said father did and four said it was mother or father, depending who was cooking. Similarly, although most children (30 out of 38) said they were asked about family holidays, they again reported that it was parents who tended to make the final decision (25 out of 38).

When it comes to 'bigger' decisions (such as moving house), children were able to provide us with many fewer examples drawn from their own experience (for example, only 10 out of 48 were able to tell us about their family's decision to move house). However, the degree to which 'democratic' processes were invoked remains very much to the fore. Nine-year-old Lloyd, who had moved 'loads of times' said:

Int.:	You've moved house have you?
L:	Yea, loads of times, I think it's about eight.
Int.:	Do they just say to you, 'Oh, we're moving house again' or do they ask you?
L:	They ask.

Lloyd, along with most other children, explained that while they were involved in the decision-making process, at this level too parents made the final decision:

Int.:	Did you all have a say in the house you were going to buy?
G:	Yes, we just said which house we wanted to go to and then it was up to my mum and dad. My mum and dad made the final decision.
Int.:	Do you think it was done in a fair way?
G:	Yea, because we all had a say in it. One got chosen in the end and I'm happy now.

Gina, aged 10

In particular circumstances, children might have a considerably greater degree of involvement and influence than might be anticipated however:

> L: One night when I came home crying my mother said to my
>   father, 'We have to move house'. And they involved me and my
>   sister and us two said, 'Yes'.
>
> Int.:   Did your mum and dad ask you where you'd like to move to?
>
> L: Yea, well they said, 'Do you wanna move from here because we
>   know you haven't got many friends?'. And we both said 'Yes'.
>   And then they asked us if we'd like to move over to Llanderyn
>   and we both said 'Yes' and we moved then.
>
> Int.:   How did mum and dad decide the house that they were going
>   to buy?
>
> L: Well, what happened was we drove around after school all the
>   streets looking to see if there were any houses up for sale.
>   Then we went to number 71 'cos they were moving, and we
>   liked that house. And we all said that we liked it and then we
>   bought it off them and then we moved in.
>
> Int.:   What do you think would have happened if you and your sister
>   [aged seven] had said no, that you didn't really like the house
>   and your mum and dad had really liked it?
>
> L: They would have went [sic] and had another look for other
>   houses.

Lee, aged 10

> H: All of us decided to move 'cos we didn't like where we were
>   staying.
>
> Int.:   Did you all go together and look at other houses?
>
> H: Yea. My mum said, 'If they choose this one and I choose that
>   one, then I'll just go with their decision'.
>
> Int.:   So the house you're moving to, did everyone like it?
>
> H: Most of us.
>
> Int.:   Who was less keen?
>
> H: My mum [laughing].
>
> Int.:   So in the end the children [Holly, her 12-year-old brother and
>   14-year-old sister] got their way?
>
> H: Yea.

Holly, aged 11

2.3 The authority of parents

So far, we have suggested that, despite a marked tendency in favour of 'democratic' (or at least participatory) decision-making processes, parents are almost invariably perceived as 'having the final say' or the casting vote, and children's accounts in the particular contexts that we have described thus far suggest that they are generally satisfied with how decisions and rules are made in their families (but see Chapter 3). In this section we explore the sources of parental authority and begin to explore the grounds on which it might be challenged.

One of the most common observations made by the children we spoke to was that they generally considered parents to be 'better' decision makers than children. Twenty-eight out of the 47 children who spoke to us on this topic said parents make better decisions; 14 of them said parents sometimes make better decisions. Only five said parents do not make better decisions.

Like Mandy, aged 10, many of the children were of the opinion that when it came to decision making, parents usually 'know best'.

> Int.: Why are parents able to make better decisions?
>
> M: Because I think they know what's best, better than us. We don't know if something's dangerous or something, but we still want it, but they make the right decisions I think.

Some children suggested that parents were better at making decisions because ultimately they had the authority and ability to enforce their decisions. In other words, that their authority derived essentially from their positions of power and their capacity to act. A few children, like Susan, aged 9, suggested that children's fear of punishment might give adults more 'power' in the decision-making process (see also Section 3.2):

> Int.: Do you think that adults are better at making decisions than children?
>
> S: Yes, because they're older.
>
> Int.: What difference does that make?
>
> S: They're smarter, they're bigger and if we don't let them win they'll smack us!

More frequently however, children felt that their parents possessed the necessary attributes (skills, life experience and knowledge) to know both how to make decisions (that is, the appropriate process) and how to choose between alternative outcomes. When asked why he thought parents made better decisions, Lee aged 10, typified the feelings of many of the children we spoke to when he explained:

> Because they're older and wiser and they know more about the world than us children because children are young and parents have got jobs and everything and they know more than us.

Kylie, aged 11, extends Lee's comments to incorporate the idea of trust in her parents' decisions:

> Int.: Do you think, on the whole, that parents make better decisions than children?
>
> K: Yea, because they make more sensible decisions than children.
>
> Int.: What is it that grown-ups can do that allows them to make better decisions than kids?
>
> K: 'Cos, like, they can be trusted more.

Simon, aged nine, felt that it was simply a quantitative matter of experience, that adults benefited from having merely made more decisions than children:

> Int.: What do you have to do to make good decisions?
>
> S: Well you need to look at all the small details.
>
> Int.: Why do you think grown-ups do that better?
>
> S: Probably because they've been doing it for longer. They've been making big decisions for longer.

In describing what they understood a 'better' decision made by an adult to imply, children most commonly invoked ideas of such decisions being 'sensible' (like Kylie, above) and 'fair'. (See Chapter 5 for a more detailed account of what is implied in the idea of 'fairness'. For our present purposes, this is to be understood as implying an 'inclusive/consultative' approach to decision making. See Section 2.2):

> Int.: Do you think that generally parents make better decisions than children?
>
> L: I think sometimes they do when they make more sensible decisions.
>
> Int.: Why are parents able to make more sensible decisions?
>
> L: Because they're older and they're more experienced.
>
> Int.: What do you think people need to make good decisions?
>
> L: To be sensible and maybe older and more mature.
>
> *Leanne, aged 11*

Int.:   Do you think parents make better decisions than children?

K: Yea, well, because they're like older, they know what's going on,
            and they're wiser and all that, and they just like know it. I think
            they, like, know more stuff. And if parents, like, make them,
            then they'll be a bit fairer. But, like, with children, it wouldn't
            be that fair.

Int.:   Why not? What would children do that would be unfair?

K: Well, if I, like, say, if I was deciding my own bedtime, and my
            mum didn't like it and she wasn't allowed to have a say, that
            wouldn't be fair on my mum. But if my mum had a say in it,
            then she would make it fair for her **and** me.

Kath, aged 10

Children were not uncritical of adults' decision-making capacities, however. A few
were aware that sometimes a parent's capacity to make decisions might be
compromised by a too-ready assumption that they possessed the necessary
background knowledge on the point at issue, or because a parent failed to operate
inclusively. Jane, aged 10, expresses the view held by a number of children who felt
that their parents sometimes made decisions on their behalf that the children felt
better qualified to make themselves.

She suggests that if adults simply asked their children about their preferred outcome
they would make better decisions:

            I think that if parents don't know what their child is thinking, I think
            that most parents think that their child is like them. Then I'm very
            different to my mother, and my mother thinks she knows what I like
            and if I don't like it, she still thinks I like it anyway. And I think that we
            make better decisions on our own behalf but we can't say. We've more
            idea about making decisions on our own behalf. If my mother asked me
            what I wanted she would know, I think, a lot more about me, even if she
            just asked me what's your favourite band. She'd know it's Busted that's
            my favourite and she wouldn't buy me Girls Aloud things.

Similarly, 11-year-old Andrew:

Int.:   Do you think parents make better decisions than
            children?

A: In some case they do and in some case they don't. 'Cos say, if
            someone's done something wrong and it wasn't their fault, and
            the mum told you off, in some cases a kid might have made a

better decision and asked it more fairly. Say 'Why did you do it?' and they could say 'Because my friend was teasing me' or something. And mum would ask but in some cases kids do make better decisions than grown-ups because they try to understand more.

Int.:   You think kids usually ask more questions, they want to understand more?

A: Yea, I think adults think they understand as soon as they've heard something that's gone wrong. They try to be fair but they think they understand straightaway.

Eleven-year-old Tim further develops the point that it is knowledge about the issue involved which qualifies a person to make a decision and not always simply their status (as parents). Tim did not believe that parents were always the 'better' decision makers, but merely suggests that the most qualified decision maker will be the one whom the issue concerns the most:

Int.:   Do you think that children make better decisions than adults? Is there anything that children can decide about?

T: Umm, it all depends on whether it's something to do with us or something to do with the parents.

When asked what skills people need to be good decision makers Jane, who clearly had well thought out views on this subject, suggested, with a considerable degree of maturity and empathy:

They've got to be able to accept other people's opinions and they've got to know a lot about the person who they're making decisions for and what the person who they're making the decision for really wants. Because if they don't know what they really like, then it's no use making a decision.
Jane, aged 10

Kay, aged 11, goes even further in suggesting that sometimes children will be in a far better position that some adults to make a decision:

Int.:   Do you think children can ever make better decisions than adults?

K: Sometimes, like when they go out.

Int.:   Why are children better at making those decisions?

K: Because they can remember what it's like when they were little.

Int.:	What do you think people need to be able to make good decisions?
K:	They need, like, to think in a children's way.
Int.:	Why would that help?
K:	I think the children would have a better idea of what they want.

We infer from these comments that, as far as children are concerned, parental authority derives not only from their parents' status (or power to act and enforce their decisions) but also from perceived competence (knowledge of what is at issue) and the possession of the right skills, experience and sense of 'fairness'. We shall see later that when children begin to think in terms of their own developing competence and of themselves as moving towards independence from their families, parental authority can come under a far greater degree of critical scrutiny (see Section 4.2). A pre-echo of this can be detected in Gina's comments in regards to decisions about clothes:

Int.:	What other things do children decide about better than their parents?
G:	Clothes, because they usually know what the fashion is and your mum just thinks that they are in fashion but they're not.

Gina, aged 10

Despite Gina and Kay's comments, most of the children to whom we spoke did not consider children in general to be competent decision makers (of the 28 out of 47 who said parents make better decisions, 11 referred to children as lacking competence), with some describing their own decisions as silly or childish. As 11-year-old Nina described:

> Kids make decisions, but they make the decisions they think are better, and others might think they're childish.

We identified a statistically significant correlation between children's reports of their competence to make decisions and their age.[3] We found that the children who reported that they were 'competent' tended to be older than those who reported they were not yet competent: no eight-year-olds, just over half of nine- and 10-year-olds, but most 11-year-olds reported that they were competent to make at least some decisions (see Jane's comments below).

In so far as some children regarded themselves and their peers as unable to come to 'sensible' decisions, they were concerned also that they might not be able to come to 'fair' (that is, inclusive) decisions either:

---

3   Significant at level $p = .03$.

> I wasn't good at decisions when I was younger. Probably because when I was younger I didn't think what people wanted. I think when you're young you don't think what people want, you think they want what you want and that's why people call you spoiled, because you always do what you want and you don't do what other people want.
>
> *Jane, aged 10*

In bridging the gap between their own assessment of their competence to make decisions and the capacity (often but not always) demonstrated by their parents to make better decisions, children were aware that they had something to learn:

> Int.: Do you think they [parents] would listen to what you had to say or not?
>
> R: I don't think they'd listen 'cos kids come up with funny things and then parents make the proper decisions. ... Well, because kids are normally making mistakes, ain't they? Well, children still have a lot to learn really, don't they, and adults already know, being their age.
>
> *Rob, aged nine*

It was clear, however, that most of the children felt that they were already engaged in the process of learning the skills they perceived necessary to become competent decision makers in adulthood. They described various ways in which they felt they were learning these skills:

> Int.: What is it do you think, that children have to do to be able to make decisions like adults?
>
> A: They see how their mothers or fathers make decisions or how the adults do things, that's the way to make decisions. 'Cos they're your parents and they tell their children how to do things properly 'cos, at the end of the day, they're there as well to set a good example, so their children can learn the way that they do it.
>
> *Alice, aged 11*

The idea that decision-making skills are generationally transmitted was also implied by Rory, aged 10, who explained:

> Int.: Do you think when you're an adult that you'll be able to make good decisions as well?
>
> R: Yea.

> Int.:   Why will you be able to make good decisions when you're an adult?
>
> R: Because everybody says I'm like my dad.

School was also seen as offering opportunities to learn the skills necessary to become competent decision makers:

> Int.:   Do you think parents make better decisions than children?
>
> J: Yea, because they're more responsible than us.
>
> Int.:   How do you get to be responsible?
>
> J: Learn things in school, learn to be responsible.
>
> *John, aged 10*

Media sources, such as television were also seen as a useful source for developing the knowledge and the skills that children needed:

> Int.:   How do you think you'll be able to make those decisions at the time?
>
> L: Well, umm, I would know more because I would watch the news, wouldn't I, and then I would be older and wiser as I said before.
>
> Int.:   Does watching the news help you make decisions?
>
> L: Yea.
>
> Int.:   How does it help you?
>
> L: Well, it's telling you about the world and what's happening, and it's also giving you information on what is happening around in the local areas and all that.
>
> *Lee, aged 10*

2.4 Mothers and fathers

Up to this point, we have referred to 'parents' in a somewhat 'generic' fashion; as though mums and dads played similar roles in the process of domestic decision making. Indeed, many of the children in our sample (44 out of 48) lived with both parents, and children consistently gave us to understand that family decisions were taken and rules were made, or at least agreed upon, by both parents:

> Int.:   Who decided where you could go with friends?
>
> J: My parents, they both did, it was a joint decision.
>
> *Jane, aged 10*

Int.: Who decided that you would have to go to bed earlier?

D: My father discussed it with my mother and my mother said it was fine.

Dan, aged 11

Int.: Who decided that ten o'clock was going to be your bedtime?

R: My mum and dad.

Int.: Who decides the rules about where you can and can't go and play with your friends?

R: My mum and my dad. With kidnappings and stuff, that's why my mum says, 'Oh, no, you're not allowed to go'.

Int.: Who usually makes the decisions that have been made in your family?

R: My dad and mum.

Rory, aged 10

It should be noted that even in the small number of families in our sample (three) where children live with one parent but spend time with the other, we were told that there was general agreement between parents over routine family decisions. (The remaining child in our sample seemed to have no contact with her father at all.)

Many of the children we spoke to simply assume that their parents agree about most everyday family decisions. When children describe instances where one parent makes a decision without consulting the other, they still regard this as tantamount to a joint process and an agreed outcome. Simon, aged nine, talked about how decisions were usually made in his family:

Int.: How do you usually make decisions in your family, who's involved?

S: All of us are. Usually my mum gets us all to sit down, as many at a time as we can, and we discuss it.

Int.: And, is it usually mum who makes the final decision?

S: Yea, but usually them together, they [mum and dad] work together to make it, but then my mum has the final say in the end usually.

Int.: Is that fair?

S: Yea, usually, 'cos we all agree in the end, eventually.

Even where the practicalities of family life mean that his parents are often called to make decisions alone, 11-year-old Tom feels confident that the outcome would be the same, whichever parent happened to be the one 'at hand':

Most of the time they make them [decisions] together. Sometimes I ask my mum to go up the shop and sometimes I ask my dad and sometimes they say yes and no but my mum and dad don't mind, they would usually agree anyway.

In principle then, most of the children in our sample would seem to regard overall decision or rule making as routinely and essentially involving both parents. However, in practice, it was equally striking that many children identify clear differences in the roles occupied by their parents in family decision making, largely along gendered lines. Decisions might be 'agreed' by both parents but not all decisions will be taken by both parents, sometimes although not always for practical reasons.

When it comes to the practicalities of day-to-day living many children regard their mothers, rather than their fathers, as the ultimate and actual source of 'domestic' authority. It is mothers who are more often described as engaging directly with children in everyday decisions and the application of general house-rules. This is most commonly explained in terms of dad having other things to do:

Int.:   Who decided on your bedtimes?
B: Mum.
Int.:   Does dad have any say in this?
B: No.
Int.:   Why is it mum's decision do you think?
B: Because my dad's always on the computer.
Beth, aged 10

Int.:   Who chooses what time you have to go bed?
G: My mum mostly. She just says, 'Time for bed'.
Int.:   Is it just your mum's decision or does your dad ever get involved?
G: He usually works at night. If my mum goes out, my sister decides. I usually go about 9.30.
Gina, aged 10 (Both Gina's parents work.)

Int.:   Who was involved in making the decision about your bedtimes?
J: My mother.
Int.:   Does dad help make the decisions?
J: I don't see my father much; he's a porter in the hospital, see.
Joe, aged 10 (Joe's mother works too.)

Like 11-year-old Nina, some children suggested that their fathers were less likely to participate in routine decision making largely because they perceived this to be mum's job:

> Int.: Were you actually told not to go to town?
>
> N: No, but my mum said that we don't really know our way around.
>
> Int.: What does your dad say?
>
> N: My dad doesn't really mind. He lets my mum take care of where I go and things like that.
>
> Int.: What sort of things would your dad make rules about?
>
> M: Umm, I think my dad would let me stay up later because it's always my mum wants me to go to bed earlier.
>
> Int.: Why do you think that is?
>
> M: I dunno. I think he just can't be bothered.
>
> Int.: What sorts of decisions does your dad make?
>
> M: I think my dad just can't be bothered and he just says yes to everything, so my mum makes most of the decisions.
>
> *Mandy, aged 10*

More generally, however, the children explained their fathers' lack of involvement in everyday decisions more in terms of pragmatics than indifference. Children's interpretation of differences in parental involvement being a matter of pragmatics was reinforced by children's accounts of fathers taking over the routine decision making role when their mother was unavailable. This typically occurred on rare occasions, for example when their mothers became ill:

> Int.: Who decides in your house what your bedtime will be?
>
> G: Umm, my mum.
>
> Int.: You said your mum decides your bedtime. Does your mum normally make the decisions in your house?
>
> G: Yea.
>
> Int.: What about your dad does he ever make any decisions?
>
> G: Yea.
>
> Int.: What kind of thing does dad decide?
>
> G: Like, if my mum was ill he'll make us tea or whatever needs doing, or tell us what time to go to bed, but he's usually up my uncle's.
>
> Int.: What about if your mum and dad are in the house together? Are there some things then that your dad decides?

G: Yea, he decides if he goes out and then he comes back and plays with us and watches a film or something and he goes on his computer and does stuff.

Glen, aged 10

However, as well as in terms of the quantum of everyday engagement in decision making, there were indications that for many children, dad's involvement tended to occur more in relation to certain types and levels of decision than in others.

When asked about the decisions his mum and dad make in his family Rory, aged 10, explained:

Well, my mum is: Why don't you wake up early? Did you brush your teeth? Did you eat? Did you have your breakfast? Did you go to bed at the right time? My dad does: Do your work properly, don't be naughty, and stuff like that.

Like Rory, a number of the children who saw their mothers as the authority in everyday family business, saw their fathers as becoming more involved in family decisions either when 'bigger' decisions had to be made or when mothers needed additional support in enforcing family rules:

Int.:   Who decided the rules about bedtime?

L: Mum.

Int.:   Did your dad have any say in that?

L: No, nothing.

Int.:   Is that quite usual in your family?

L: Yea, mum usually makes the decisions, like bedtime, TV, pyjamas. Dad is more, like, the family issues like holidays – much bigger.

Lauren, aged 10

Int.:   Who decided your bedtime should be eight o'clock?

S: My mother.

Int.:   Just on her own or did your father help make that decision?

S: No [laughs]. My mother on her own.

Int.:   Why do you think it's mostly mum who makes the rules?

S: Because my dad, he's got too much work to do and stuff, so he won't interfere in stuff for the children unless it's something like going on holiday.

Shaun, aged 10 (Shaun's mother also works.)

There is evidence too that fathers play a greater part in decisions that occupy the boundary between the domestic and the public spheres, such as those relating to a child's choice of friends, curfews and where children can go unaccompanied. The contrast between what mums and dads decide in this respect was often directly pointed out by children with whom we spoke, like nine-year-old Jon and 10-year-old Jo, for example:

Int.:	What sort of things does dad make the final decision on?
Jon:	Where we're going on Saturday and umm ... if we're going to stay in on rainy days.
Int.:	Does mum make final decisions about things?
Jon:	Yea, like what we're going to have for food.
Int.:	What kind of decisions does your dad make?
Jo:	If we have a day off from school, what we'd do and where we'd go, and my mum decides what we have for tea.

This distinction may in part be concerned with the slightly enhanced role assigned to fathers in relation to 'bigger' decisions and in the enforcement of joint parental decisions but it may also be suggestive of the persistence of traditional gender roles in parenting in the families of the children with whom we spoke. We are unable to develop this point further as we did not gather data from parents on this point.

2.5 Key findings

- Decision making within families is subtle, complex and dynamic.
- It rarely relies on explicit, formal, decision-making events or protocols.
- It is a cumulative process which produces a stock of 'common knowledge' within families that grows over time.
- Processes for reaching decisions vary within and between families.
- For most families, in matters small and large, these processes tend towards the democratic/participatory but parents are usually regarded, by consent, as having ultimate authority.
- Children can however be the decisive influence, even in major decisions.
- The authority of parents is understood by children to derive from their competence and life experience (rather than their status as parents).
- Children tend to trust their parents to make 'good decisions'.
- 'Good' decisions are those that are well informed and fair (inclusive).
- Children vary in the degree to which they regard themselves as competent decision makers.

- Children regard themselves as in the process of learning how to make 'better decisions' and see themselves as increasingly competent decision makers.
- Children generally regard their parents as making decisions or rules on which both parents do or would agree.
- Decisions might be 'agreed' by both parents but not all decisions will be taken or carried into effect by both parents equally.
- In fact, mothers are more usually the ultimate and actual source of domestic authority.
- Fathers are less actively involved in making domestic decisions, except where these affect the whole family (or when the domain of decision making begins to move outside of the home).

3. Making your own way: Negotiating involvement in family life

3.1 Introduction

We have indicated already that decision making in families is rarely an explicit process. Decisions are reached as part of a complex interplay between parents and their children that tends towards the inclusive and rests on the assumed competence of those involved. As such, general rules and specific decisions are widely followed and accepted by children, as we have suggested. They are part of their familial micro-culture to which they naturally adapt. This is particularly so, it would appear, for younger children, who are still positioned at the dependant, family-oriented/'we-feeling' end of a continuum that runs, with age, towards independence and self-actualisation/'I-feeling', and who tend to occupy domestic much more than public space.

As such, we find comparatively little evidence of children seeking to negotiate variations in family rules as far as decisions operating at the level of everyday routines or whole-family life are concerned. There is more evidence of negotiation and of a weakening consensus where decisions are concerned with the child's developing sense of individuality, autonomy and independence or self-actualisation, however. These are explored in detail in Chapter 4.

3.2 Limits to negotiation

Parental authority is self-evident to many children and largely unquestioned:[4]

> J: Yea, if I talk to my mother then she'll probably listen to me, but I don't know if she'll agree with me because, umm, she's strong-willed.

---

4 One might note, in passing, how for most of the situations and issues described by children in this chapter, 'mum' is almost universally regarded as the actual maker of decisions and rules (see Section 2.4).

Int.:   If she doesn't agree with what you say, what would you imagine would happen?

J: I would imagine that we would carry on like before, because she is my mother and you gotta respect her decision, that's what I think.

Jane, aged 10

Int.:   If your parents make a decision and you disagree, what would happen?

G: It's their way.

Int.:   Is there anything you can do or do you not bother?

G: Say the good things about them and say the bad things. It sometimes works.

Int.:   Who gets the final decision?

G: My mum.

Gina, aged 10

Int.:   If you disagreed about something, what would you do? Would you try and change their minds?

S: Yea.

Int.:   How would you try and change their minds? What would you do?

S: Start arguing [giggles] and then they'd get madder and madder and madder and madder until the argument went mad.

Int.:   What normally happens? Who normally wins the argument?

S: Mum.

Int.:   Why does mum win? What does she do to win?

S: She's a parent [indignantly].

Int.:   What difference does that make?

S: 'Cos they're a bit strong. I'm a child, I'm not as strong as them. That's mostly it.

Shaun, aged 10

As nine-year-old Susan indicated earlier (see Section 2.3), for some children parental authority can be reinforced through punishment, although we found that children said very little about the use of punishment in the enforcement of family rules.

The prospect of family disharmony is also a factor for some children when a rule or decision is at issue. Stewart, aged 10, is careful not to go too far:

Int.:	What would you do, if you wanted to go out and play somewhere, how would you try and change her mind?
S:	That's impossible.
Int.:	Do you ever get to change mum's mind?
S:	No.
Int.:	If you disagree with something that your parents say, would you tend to keep quiet or would you try and change their mind?
S:	Keep quiet. 'Cos we'll just end up arguing and mum and dad'll end up shouting at me.
Int.:	Who normally gets the final decision?
S:	Them.

For 10-year-old Lee, the prospect of punishment and a family row amounts to much the same thing, although interestingly it is by no means unusual for the children to whom we spoke, to want to take a less conflictual approach:

Int.:	Why is it you don't like getting annoyed with your parents, is it because you don't like having a row or is it because of what punishment you might get?
L:	The punishment. I also don't wanna really get into a row with my mother and my father.
Int.:	Why not?
L:	Because I don't like hearing them shouting; I just like to talk.

3.3 Points of departure

A general acceptance of the authority of parents and of the 'rules of the house' does not mean that there are no points of disagreement however. Given the emergent nature of a family's 'rules', and notwithstanding our observation (see Section 2.3) that 'rules' obtain their authority from the competence as much as the status of the rule maker (parent), specific applications of the 'rules' or other points of decision can sometimes appear to a child to be capricious, if not arbitrary.

In relation to domestic, private matters, minor conduct rules, such as bedtimes, are sometimes variable in their application, for no apparent reason, according to 11-year-old Tim:

Sometimes I feel that way, like I wanna go to bed a bit later. Well it's usually like when I'm watching something good on TV and I'm like, 'Can I stay up a bit later and watch the end of this?' Sometimes they say

'No, you've gotta go to bed now' or sometimes, like, 'Five more minutes' or 'Ten more minutes'.

The application of 'rules' can appear to owe more to the passing mood of a parent, especially (and understandably) towards the end of the day:

Int.:	Do you always have to ask if you can stay up a bit later?
J:	I have to ask. I ask if I could watch the end or can I watch it until the next advert.
Int.:	What does mum normally say?
J:	She says yes sometimes but if she's in a bad mood she just sends me to bed.

Jo, aged 10

A request for a ruling can also be expressed in terms of a very familiar parental equivocation:

Int.:	Could you get your parents to agree to you going to Pontwyn, could you make then change their minds?
J:	I have tried. I asked my father if I was allowed to go. He either says 'We'll see' or he says 'No'.

Josie, aged 10

More often, the application of a rule, or more precisely, permission to bend or relax a rule, is dependent, not on the merits of the case, the particular rule in question or even the mood of the rule maker, but on the context in which the case is considered. Most often, the context is whether the child has been 'good' or not.

Talking about bedtimes again:

J:	Well sometimes if I'm watching a film I ask my mother if I can stay late to watch the end. Sometimes she says 'No, it's too late' and sometimes she says 'Yes, you can stay up'.
Int.:	What does it depend on?
J:	It depends on what my behaviour's like. If I was naughty then she'd say, 'No, you're naughty today, you gotta go to bed early'.

Jill, aged nine

S:	Umm, yea, because, my mum says I can read until nine but I'd like to read a bit further, like quarter past or something.
Int.:	Have you ever suggested that to her?
S:	Yea.

Int.:   What did she say?

S: She sometimes says 'Yes' and she sometimes says 'No'.

Int.:   Do you know when she might be more likely to say yes?

S: When I've been good all day.

Sara, aged 10

The following quotation, while demonstrating once again how contextual rather than situational a contested or negotiated decision around bedtime is, also suggests how children attempt to influence decision making by influencing the context, that is, by being 'good':

N: But sometimes, if we're really good, mum will let us stay up a bit later, if she's in the mood, if we haven't had a busy day.

Int.:   Do you ever try and stay up a bit later?

N: [Laughs] Everyone does that.

Int.:   What do you do to try and stay up a bit later?

N: We're good.

Natasha, aged nine

In persuading his parents to let him go with his friends to the local shops, 10-year-old John clearly knows how to prepare the ground:

Int.:   If you asked several times a week to go to the shop, would she let you go every time you asked?

J: No.

Int.:   What would it depend on?

J: If I'd been good or not probably.

Int.:   What else can you do to make your mum let you have your own way?

J: Do chores, or take out the rubbish, take the bin down to the kerb, clean my bedroom.

Sara, aged 10, whom we reported earlier trying to extend her bedtime reading, when asked how she would get her parents to agree to her having her light on longer, explained:

Umm ... because me and my brother are always fighting, so be a bit more behaved and be more gentle to him, because I'm that bit rough sometimes.

It would seem the case that negotiations around the application of rules are more commonly conducted through attempts to manipulate the context in which a specific rule is being applied. Sometimes, as we have seen, this involves 'being good'. It can also involve the opposite with a common form of negotiation being a kind of emotional attrition. For example, while Shaun (above) may try and start an argument, 10-year-old Lee opts for a campaign of:

> ... hassle and moan ...

Eleven-year-old Kay adopts a tactic of:

> ... nagging and hanging around ...

While Rory, aged 10, favours either crying to get his own way or simply:

> ... standing and looking sad ...

And 10-year-old Jo may:

> ... try and say something really horrible ...

Children recognise that it is unwise to push this tactic too far and need to be capable of switching modes, as 10-year-old Mandy explained:

M:	'Cos if I just keep asking the same question, after a while she just goes, 'Ok'.
Int.:	So you just keep on and on asking?
M:	Yea. Every five minutes. Every time I remember it, I just ask. But if my mum's giving me something like, oh, we're going to town to buy some new stuff, I don't really mention it 'cos I know she's gonna say, 'Right, that's it, you're not having anything'. I just ask her every ... if I really want it then, like, I'll just leave it and I tidy up stuff and after a while she says, 'Alright, then'.
Int.:	When you say you tidy up stuff you mean you try to be good, you try to be helpful?
M:	Yea.
Int.:	What difference do you think that makes?
M:	I'm being good, but I know that if I keep doing it only when I want something, then I should do it all the time anyway.

It is a fine line between being instrumental in one's actions (acting with a purpose) and being manipulative (acting out of a narrow self-interest). The latter has unwelcome moral overtones and, as a term of disapprobation or even rebuke, is sometimes applied to children's behaviour. We note that parents, apparently, endorse this strategy in so far as they too seem prepared to use indirect negotiation to achieve their desired ends. It is parents who make their decision dependent upon the child's behaviour.

The inference we draw from the preceding quotations is simply that children are conscious agents in this process of 'indirect' negotiation with their parents. Their responses suggest self-conscious agency if not direct intent. They suggest reflection more than reaction. What this also emphasises is how important it is for the child to have an intimate understanding of the context (the family micro-culture) in which he or she is operating. The child needs to know what style of behaviour to adopt (being good or the opposite) depending on the parent and the situation at issue, and needs to know the limits and the point of diminishing returns. This intimate knowledge of the context suggests to us the importance of a shared history and a reasonably predictable set of expectations of the conduct of others in the family.

Children tend to be quicker to defend their right to disagree explicitly and to argue their position more openly in relation to decisions that we have characterised as being to do with self-actualisation (see Chapter 4 for a more substantial discussion of this point). These discussions are often conducted in terms of clothes, personal space or going out with friends:

> Int.: If mum knows best, why's it important to have a say in what you wear?
>
> J: Because it's about me, so I should get a say.
> *Jo, aged 10*

Appearance is not necessarily a gendered issue, as 11-year-old Oliver makes clear:

> Int.: What about having to wear school uniform? Is it a good thing?
>
> O: No, I just think we should decide what we want to choose. If you wear what they want... you'd want to have like your own personal ... 'cos, like, sometimes if you wear particular clothes it says something about you, but if you didn't like school clothes ... I think they're a bit dull.
>
> Int.: Is it important to you how you look?
>
> O: It's important that I get to choose because it's me. If my parents always chose it would be boring because you may not even like the clothes and they might say that you have to wear them.
>
> Int.: What if your mum was choosing clothes for you every day. How would you feel about that?
>
> O: Really annoyed and I would argue; that's one thing I would argue about.

Leanne, aged 11, is also prepared to take a stand in the face of parental opposition, it would appear:

> L: Say I was wearing a nice top, then she'd just say to 'Go and change it and just put on a normal top to go round the park'.
>
> Int.: And what would you do?
>
> L: I'd go and change.
>
> Int.: How would you feel if your mum chose all of your clothes for you?
>
> L: I wouldn't like it, and I probably wouldn't wear them either.

Eleven-year-old Jenny is even more positive and explicitly makes the issue one of identity and personal integrity:

> Int.: What happens if mum wants you to have something you don't like?
>
> J: I just say 'No, I don't wanna wear it', and I won't wear it. Yea, because it's, like, my body that I'm covering, and I should feel comfortable in the clothes I wear, and it should be my decision.

Ellie is quite prepared to lie to her parents to see her friends. This is despite a strong presumption against lying to parents described by some children.

> Int.: What happens if she says, 'No, you can't go out with your friends'?
>
> E: I just go mad. I just start performing and I just tries [sic] to go.
>
> Int.: What are the things you do to try and change her mind?
>
> E: I say I'm going somewhere else and I'll be back in an hour, and she still says no.
>
> Int.: Is it easy to change your mother's mind?
>
> E: No. Difficult.
>
> *Ellie, aged 11*

Oliver, whose views on school uniform and personal appearance we heard earlier, would appear prepared to take more direct action:

> Int.: She tells you when your clothes need changing?
>
> O: Sometimes I'd say, 'Yea, ok', then I'll go and get changed and sometimes I just walk out. Because we've got three doors I can just go out.
>
> *Oliver, aged 11*

Ten-year-old Lauren, while recognising her mum's authority, is, in conversation with us, determinedly defiant. We return to some of Lauren's comments on negotiation below. The following is the expression of a decided resistance to accepting her parents' authority:

Int.:   Do you think it's important that you get to decide what you wear?

L: Yes it is 'cos, like, if I don't want to wear a pink frilly top I'm not going to wear it even if my mum says it. I'm just not going to wear it because, I don't mind the colour pink, just not frilly and everything.

3.4 Talking it through

We encountered very few examples of a child and his or her parents directly 'talking through' a point of disagreement in what appeared to be an equitable way:

Int.:   When you're at your dad's house, can you change things to be done fairly?

J: Yea.

Int.:   What do you do?

J: I try and tell him, and then he listens to me and then ... umm ... he talks to his girlfriend about it then, and then if they both agree they talk to me and tell me what they've said and everything.

Julie, aged nine

More commonly, active negotiation on the child's part reflected the tensions between the child's desire for increasing autonomy and a recognition that parents possessed 'ultimate' authority. This sometimes produced a degree of subversion on the child's part (in which parents are often complicit) and, in the end, a modest degree of independent action on the part of the child. Lauren, whom we heard earlier, making it clear that she would not wear anything 'frilly', echoes many of the themes of this chapter when she describes the pattern of negotiation between herself and her parents:

Int.:   Were you able to change that rule?

L: Yea, I used to only be allowed to go with someone older than me but now at least it's with one friend or two.

Int.:   How did you manage to change their minds about that?

L: I just said, 'I'm not your little girl any more', and that sort of thing. 'I'm 10 now and not five years old.' They just keep giving road safety, that's all they're bothered about.

Int.:   If you disagree with something, do you just go along with it or try and change their minds?

L: I try and change their minds, but if they are really specific in what they want then there's no stopping them really, even if you try to change their minds. Dad is easy to change but mum is a tough one.

Int.:   What do you do?

L: Well, I might say, 'Well, think about us as well. We're your children aren't we, don't you love us?', you try and say that sort of thing. Sometimes it does work but hardly ever. They do like what's best for us so that's why we usually get to have a say in it, but they don't believe in hitting and say, 'No you're not having it' and snap, they explain to you. Yes but when I was little I was hanging upside down in the bath on the rail and dad said 'You shouldn't do that' and he gave half an hour's talking and I went back on and I hung upside-down again and he gave an even longer ... and I said, 'Yes I understand' and went back on swinging up and down, so dad just gave up then. If I keep doing what I want then eventually he'll give up.

Lauren, aged 10

While we found little evidence of children's direct experience of explicit verbal negotiation, some children would have liked the opportunity to gather experience of this kind, recognising its value as part of preparing for later childhood and adolescence. Ten-year-old Jane, whom we heard earlier talking about the respect that is due to her mother, still recognised that she would need the skills that such negotiations might bring:

J: I think my mother should agree more to what I say, because sometimes we do have arguments about what I wanna do at a certain time and sometimes we just can't agree.

Int.:   Why should she agree with you?

J: I think that I should have a say in what my life at home's like because if I, like, one day I'm going to be like a grown-up then I'm gonna have decisions, but if I don't make decisions when I'm younger then I won't know what to do.

Age was an important factor for most children when considering their capacity to engage more successfully in decision making. Most often, children saw their capacity for influence and autonomy increasing with age. However, rarely was the specific age identified – it was almost always a few years over the horizon. We return to the topic of age and competence at Section 4.5.

3.5 Key findings

- Children generally accept the authority of parents.
- The limits to challenging parental authority are, to a very minor degree, set by the fear of punishment and the wish of the child to avoid conflict.
- Where differences over everyday family life arise, direct negotiation between parents and children is uncommon.
- Given that parental authority rests on competence as much as status, some decisions appear arbitrary or capricious to children.
- Such decisions are more likely to be 'contextual' rather than situationally specific, often drawing in a consideration of whether a child has been 'good' or not.
- Hence, children's attempts to re-negotiate such decisions are also likely to be indirect (rather than focusing on the issue in question) and will often involve 'contextual' tactics such as being good, hassling and moaning.
- Such subtle negotiations would seem to rely on an intimate knowledge of the adults involved and their likely reactions.
- Indirect negotiations of this sort suggest a degree of self-conscious agency on the part of children and a degree of adaptation or reflection (rather than reaction), such that children know the limits of their capacity to engage successfully in 'negotiations' of this sort.
- Some parents may be complicit in children's 'indirect negotiations'.
- Children can switch modes easily and generally do not seek confrontation.
- Children are more likely to resist parental authority in relation to decisions concerning self-actualisation.
- In such circumstances, children will break other rules, for example by lying, and may be openly defiant.

4. Going your own way: Making autonomous decisions

4.1 Introduction

We have sought to imply that the process of family decision making is an osmotic one that builds to a shared, 'cultural' appreciation of the family's norms and expectations. In our view therefore, it is perhaps not surprising that the children to whom we spoke generally make few claims to autonomous decision making (see also Sections 2.2 and 2.3). Moreover, where children are inclined to defer to parental authority and competence and to regard themselves as 'not-yet-competent', the children we spoke to, with some exceptions (discussed below), did not regard themselves as substantially disenfranchised. As 10-year-old Lee explained:

> Int.: Do you think at some point you'll make decisions on your own?
>
> L: Yea, but I'd ask my mother and father as soon as I know my decision.
>
> Int.: When do you think you might start make decisions on your own?
>
> L: Well, when I'm older and wiser really.
>
> Int.: How old do you think you'd have to be to start making decisions on your own?
>
> L: About 20 or 21.
>
> Int.: Would you like to be able to decide things on your own?
>
> L: No, not really now. Because I don't know what would be right or what would be wrong, so I need to gather my thoughts first before I make a decision.

This is not to say however, that a few children did not feel as though there were important areas of family decision making from which they had been excluded, as we shall report. Moreover, the distinction we observed in the previous section between decisions made concerning domestic space and personal conduct and those that were to do with an awakening sense of self and personal identity (as distinct from an identity within the family) was clearly echoed in what talk there was about 'making one's own decisions'.

4.2 Doing your own thing

Where children did lay claim to making autonomous decisions (25 out of 45 children), they were often to do with essentially minor conduct matters such as how they allocated their own leisure and play time, subject to the limits established by the family's norms; whether to watch TV or play; what time to have a bath; or, in relation to minor treats, what to have from the ice cream van or what they wanted for Christmas. These were, according to 10-year-old Jane:

> ... only small decisions ... [that a] one-year-old could make ...

As noted however, self-presentation (clothes) was the subject of some very definite claims to independence and autonomy as well as to identity (see Section 3.3):

Int.:	Do you ever make any decisions on your own?
J:	Yea, like what I wear. Like, if my mum asked me what I wanted, I would decide that.
Int.:	Is it important that you can make some decisions on your own?
J:	Yea, because I should have my say, because it would be about me.

Jo, aged 10

> Because it's my stuff that I'm gonna actually wear. If mum was gonna wear it, then it's up to her, but if I was gonna wear it then it's up to me what I wear.
>
> *Mandy, aged 10*

Bedrooms too emerged as an important physical representation of some children's developing sense of independent identity. Ten-year-old Gina is very clear about what her room means to her:

Int.:	Do you ever make decisions completely on your own?
G:	Yes, my room. When I want to refurbish.
Int.:	Is that important to you?
G:	Yes 'cos it's my territory. It's my room, they've got to at least ask me and it's the one place where I can have some peace and quiet without the shouting.

Making your bedroom your 'own' was important to children, even if this led to the potential for disagreements with parents:

Int.:   Is there anything that you're not allowed a say in that you'd really like a say in?

D: Umm, stuff to go in my bedroom ... furniture. When they buy furniture and then got to move the old furniture, sometimes they put it in my bedroom and they don't ask if I want it moving in there.

Int.:   Is it fair that your parents do that?

D: No, because they put the stuff there without asking me if I mind.

Dan, aged 11

For 10-year-old Mandy, the eldest of four sisters, her bedroom was the place where she could make the rules, or would have liked to:

M: Yea, but if it's a bit messy, my mum always tidies my bedroom up for me. I don't mind. But I like to tidy it myself sometimes, 'cos I have some stuff that I don't want her looking at and stuff, so I like tidying it myself.

Int.:   Is it important that you've got your own space?

M: Yea, space.

Int.:   Why is that important?

M: I dunno. I just have stuff I don't wanna tell them sometimes.

Int.:   Do you makes rules about things that they're not allowed to do?

M: Yea. But my dad always, like, teases me and comes in and has a look anyway. And I push him out the way 'cos I wanna keep it to myself.

Int.:   What are the rules you have for your parents?

M: They're not allowed in. I'm having a lock on my bedroom soon 'cos my mother keeps saying to my dad I can have a lock if he keeps coming in.

Int.:   Does your mum stay out?

M: Yea.

Int.:   What's the rule?

M: They knock on my door usually.

Int.:   Then they have to ask if they can come in?

M:	Yea. Or sometimes I say, 'Alright, come in a minute' and put away what I want or something.
Int.:	And is it important that you can make your own rules about that?
M:	Yea, because it's my bedroom and it's my stuff, ain't it?
Int.:	Do they listen to your decisions?
M:	My mum does but I don't think my dad always listens.
Int.:	And what do you think about that?
M:	I don't like it because it's my stuff and sometimes he teases me a lot. He keeps laughing and calling me stuff, like. He's only joking, but sometimes I don't like him seeing stuff.

Choice of friends too was something that children wished to reserve to themselves. As nine-year-old Natasha explained:

Int.:	Are there any decisions which you make completely on your own, for yourself?
N:	My friends. Mum and dad can't stop me from being with anyone. I don't think it's fair if your mum and dad pick your friends.
Int.:	Why isn't it fair?
N:	They didn't stop me from playing with Ewan, because mum and dad like Ewan; they say he's nice. And my brother's friend, Dan, they say he's nice.
Int.:	Is it important to you that you get to choose something like your own friends?
N:	Yea, 'cos, well, your mum and dad just can't stop you from playing with your friends. And say your mum picks your friends, you're gonna get bored with them, really, ain't you? And what if it was someone that was, like, your enemy?

4.3 Wanting more of a say?

A quarter of the children to whom we spoke (12) explicitly stated that they would wish to have greater involvement in their family's decision making. Most of these were only looking for room to negotiate in those areas already negotiated by many children (bedtimes, bath times, play times and the like).

There was also some interest in a greater degree of influence in 'family decisions' such as the purchase of a car, where to go on holiday or buying a new TV. It is interesting to note that, in each of these instances, the children's families scored highly (positively) on the scale that we used to measure cohesion and expressiveness (see Appendix 1.4.2). It may be that where children live in families that have a sense of common purpose and which routinely talk about family business, children's expectations of being included in family decision making rise accordingly.

In a small number of cases, it was clear that children had felt excluded from important family business, however. Two cases in particular are suggestive of continuing difficulties in the families concerned. Joe, aged 10, describes patterns of communication in his family as generally poor. He noted that he and his mother agree only 'sometimes' and that he and his father do not agree at all. He would have liked much more involvement than appeared to be on offer to him (see Appendix 1.4.3). In response to being asked if there were areas of family life in which he would like to have a say, he replied:

J:	My family's health. Like, umm ... my family, if they have had a row or something and I don't know about it, or if they're keeping secrets from each other.
Int.:	Why don't you have a say?
J:	Umm ... 'cos I think my family don't want to put too much pressure on me 'cos I'm only 10 and they think I should be older.

(For further details of Joe's relationship with his parents see Section 5.2).

Eleven-year-old Jenny described the pattern of communication in her family in broadly similar terms to Joe, although her relationship with her father she regarded somewhat more positively and she did report that her mother 'always' knew her thoughts and feelings. However, even though there appears to be a closer understanding between Jenny and her mother, the outstanding issue is her mother's working hours:

Int.:	Are there decisions you don't get to take part in?
J:	Mmm, yea. Like what time my mum goes to work. She's always in work. I know my mum's got to work. And she has to work so she can take me places, like on Saturday night and things.
Int.:	Do you think it's fair that she has to work to take you places?
J:	Yea, but she always works, like, she always works just when I come home from school, she goes to work. And she always goes

> out on Friday nights with her friends. Sometimes she goes on
> Wednesdays and Saturdays too.

Int.:   Do you mind that?

J: No, not' really, because I'm still with my dad. But I'd like her
to, like, stay home more. 'Cos I watch telly and I see all of these
people that have kids, and their mums like stay home. And
they have them like 24/7. But my mum don't [sic], she like
goes to work and my dad doesn't come home 'til five o'clock,
so some days I'm all by myself.

The sense in which being left out of decisions on important family business can cause anxieties has been reported by us elsewhere (Butler and others 2003) and is by no means confined to families experiencing difficulties. Ten-year-old Lee's family scores very nearly at the top of the range for cohesiveness and expressiveness, and he describes patterns of communication within his family in very positive terms (see Appendix 1.4.2 and 1.4.3). Indeed, Lee's description of his family life was as positive a presentation as we found among the children to whom we spoke. We have heard Lee already tell us that he is generally content to consult with his parents, yet he described the following incident to us:

Int.:   Are there any other things that you would like to have a say in?

L: No not really. Only, like, when my auntie had died and I would
have liked to have gone to see her gravestone, but they
wouldn't have let me.

Int.:   Did you go to the funeral?

L: No, they wouldn't let me.

Int.:   Would you have liked to have gone to the funeral?

L: Yea.

Int.:   Did they ask you whether you'd like to go along?

L: No.

Int.:   What did you think about that at the time?

L: Well, I thought she's my auntie and I want to pay my last
respects too.

Int.:   Did you tell your mum and dad that?

L: No.

Int.:   Why not?

L: Because I keep quiet and I, umm, don't like to have rows and
all that.

(For a striking parallel see Butler and Williamson 1994: 52. For further details of Lee's relationship with his parents see Section 5.2).

We directly matched each child's responses to the questions: 'How involved do you feel in family issues?' and 'How much do you want to be involved in family issues?' (see Appendix 1.4.3). From this we found that 19 children wanted a greater degree of involvement than they currently perceived was to be available to them, 23 felt they had the right degree of involvement while six felt they wanted to be less involved than they currently felt they were. The discrepancy between the degree of involvement that children want and that is available to them, has been noted in other circumstances (see, for example, Butler and others 2003).

Exploring involvement further, we found only one statistically significant association between involvement and the demographic, child–parent communication and family functioning variables we assessed (see Appendix 1). In keeping with our earlier observation (see Section 4.3), this association was between child involvement and family 'expressiveness'.[5] Overall, there was a tendency for children who wanted to be 'very much' involved to score their family high (positively) on 'expressiveness'. Further analysis showed that there were no other inter-correlations between 'expressiveness' and other of the demographic or child–parent communication variables we assessed, including social class.

As well as noting the convergence between involvement wanted and that available, it is interesting to note also the divergence: the range of responses given by children. It is important to note that some children do not want to be involved at all in the decision-making processes in their family, and some want less involvement than others. At a time when there is a great deal of professional interest in child development (see, for example, the *Framework for the Assessment of Children in Need*, DH 2000), it is important to guard against any generalising tendency that an uncritical appreciation of 'developmentalism' may produce.

4.4 One day ...

Most children had a sense that with increasing age would come increasing 'responsibility':

Int.:	Do you think the decision about your bedtimes will be made differently when you're 11?
J:	Yea, because I'll be older and I can make the right choice better.
Int.:	What's going to help you make the right choice?
J:	I'll be more responsible 'cos I'm older.

---

5   Significant at level p = .03.

> Int.:   So, if you don't get your way about where you can go, is that unfair?
>
> J: No, no, 'cos I'm not really responsible now, I'm only 10.
>
> *John, aged 10*

With increasing age and 'responsibility' (perhaps in the sense of experience and competence), a greater degree of independent decision making would follow in the expectations of most children. Eleven-year-old Oliver, whom we encountered earlier contemplating taking fairly direct action if he were to be prevented from 'going out' (see Section 3.3), clearly articulated his expectations that, with age also, would come an increasing right to engage in the decision-making process:

> Int.:   Do you think things will change in terms of how things are decided and how independent you are over the next three years or so?
>
> O: Yea.
>
> Int.:   Is it changing already?
>
> O: Kind of yes. I talk more with them and I think they understand a bit more.
>
> Int.:   Do you think they listen to you more?
>
> O: Yes.
>
> Int.:   Why?
>
> O: Because you're older and people kind of listen to you more. I don't know why really because they should all listen.
>
> Int.:   You don't think it should necessarily be because of your age?
>
> O: No, if you're too young, like five or six, it would be harder for them to understand, but I think they should still talk about it. Every person is equal really, different ages, but they should try and talk when they're five or six but it would be hard for them sometimes. They should talk a bit and ask loads and loads of questions and if they don't understand they should ask. They should ask questions because that makes you know more, but if they had loads and loads of questions that wouldn't be so good.

There is a suggestion in Oliver's account of a degree of tension in asking enough but not too many questions. It is interesting to note that he rates his family high in terms of cohesion but high also in terms of levels of conflict and relatively low in terms of expressiveness (see Appendix 1.4.2).

For Oliver, along with most other children, the right age at which one might begin to have more of a 'say' was just over the horizon:

Int.:   Is it important to you that you get to decide on your own?

O: Yea, because then your life isn't controlled and when you're older you'd be more independent.

Int.:   Do you think you will become more independent when you get older?

O: Yea.

Int.:   What age do you think you'll be?

O: Thirteen or 14 because I'm older and I'll be allowed to do more stuff and decide what to do.

Oliver's older brother was aged 13 and it was the case that entering their teens was a definite transitional point for a number of children to whom we spoke. As 10-year-old Gina made clear, when you are a teenager:

> You can like go off and do your own thing and then you can have your own opinion.

Ten-year-old Lauren explained:

Int.:   So you could have the final say in what you wear?

L: Yea.

Int.:   Do you think that will happen one day?

L: Maybe when I'm old enough. Mum keeps saying, 'I don't care what you wear when you move out'. But I'll probably have the final say when I'm fifteen or something, 'cos by then I'll be able to put my foot down and say, 'Look mum I'm not doing that' and that's what teenagers do anyway.

Lauren was not entirely confident that getting to 15 would be enough however. She went on to say:

Int.:   When do you think you'll be making more decisions entirely on your own?

L: When I move out, probably when I'm in university. When I'm in comprehensive I might make decisions entirely on my own more often, not completely.

Int.:   Why in comprehensive? What difference will that make?

L: I'm older, I'll have had more experience. That's what my parents tell me most of the time. They always say that I don't have to do exactly as they say. Like, they keep saying, 'You don't have to wear that, it's your life', 'You don't have to not go out with that boy', that sort of thing.

Others did not use such transitional points as moving school (or going to university!) but, like Oliver, took their measure from their older brothers or sisters.

4.5 Siblings

Given that the majority of children in our sample had at least one sibling (46 out of 48 children), it is not surprising that children's accounts of family decision making include a great deal of reference to their brothers and sisters who had a marked impact on progress towards being able to 'go one's own way'; particularly in the way that reference to the experience of older brothers and sisters offered a 'map' of their own future.

Decision making and rule construction are, as we have suggested, rarely explicit processes in families. Similarly, children's experiences of being involved with their siblings in an explicit decision-making process only usually occurred when very particular decisions had to be made, such as 'where we go on holiday'. In these circumstances the children reported having to negotiate with their siblings, as well as other family members. Typically this was done through majority voting (with parents usually having the casting vote, as we have noted) and taking turns in order to reach family agreement about the best outcome (see Section 2.2). As a result, having siblings sometimes meant having to compromise on one's preferred outcome or being prepared to wait for one's turn. We were impressed with how many children, like Jane, aged 10, showed a willingness to compromise for the sake of siblings, particularly younger ones:

> J: I think my sister [aged two] kind of stops things because she's so young and she can't do certain things. We have to go and see a young film.
>
> Int.: How do you feel about that, do you think it's fair?
>
> J: I think it is fair at the moment because my sister can't help the age she is, and I'm an 11-year-old. And she's still my sister and even though she is a pain she's still my sister.

(Although Jane refers to herself as an '11-year-old', when we interviewed her she was 10; her birthday she explained was 'next week'.)

In addition, the children sometimes demonstrated a parental kind and level of concern for their younger siblings over issues of safety and well-being when involved in family decision making of this nature:

Int.:	How about your brother [aged six] and sisters [aged seven and eight], are there different rules for them about playing with friends?
R:	Yes, because they're only small and they're not allowed out but only with my mum and dad or a grown-up, because for their own safety and so they don't get lost.
Int.:	Do you remember it being like that when you were their age?
R:	Yes.
Int.:	When did it change for you?
R:	About seven.
Int.:	Do you think it will change for them?
R:	I don't know, I think so yes, when they're about nine.
Int.:	Do you think it's fair that you're allowed to do things they're not allowed to do?
R:	Yes. They're only small and I'm 10 and so if they go out someone has to take them out.

Ruhana, aged 10

It was with older siblings however, that interest among the young people we spoke to was highest. For most children the rules that applied to older siblings were seen as setting a useful precedent for understanding what might happen to themselves in the future. Ellen, aged nine, described how she believed that her bedtime would change when she reaches the same age as her sisters:

Int.:	What do you think about the fact that you and your sisters all have different bedtimes?
E:	I think it's quite fair because people who are older don't normally feel as tired as people who are younger, so maybe they can make their own decisions more.
Int.:	Do you think by the time you get to Isobel's age [13] and then Amy's [16] that you'll get to stay up the same time as them?
E:	Yea.
Int.:	Do you think that's important that you'll be treated the same as them at their age, or doesn't it matter?
E:	It's sort of important 'cos if I got, like, an earlier time and I was their age now, it wouldn't really be fair.

Like Ellen, 10-year-old Josie and nearly all of the children to whom we spoke, worked on the assumption that rules that applied to their older siblings would apply to them when they reached the same age:

> Int.: Do you think where you're allowed to go with friends will ever change?
>
> J: Yea. When I get older, my sister's age [12].

Kath, aged 10, looked forward to the day when she is allowed to have her friends around in the way that her older brother does:

> Because, like, my brother's 16 and he just, like, phones his friends to come over. And they just, like, come in and stay there, like for ages. But I'm not really allowed to do that, yet [laughs].

It was apparent that children also used these precedents as tools for negotiation when engaged in the rule/decision-making process with their parents.

Just as the children we talked to expected the same treatment at the same age as their older siblings, they also expected their younger siblings to be treated as they were at a given age.

> Int.: What about your brother [aged eight], does he have the same rules as you?
>
> L: Well, I started going to the park when I was 10 and he'll be allowed to go and play with his friends then if he's sensible enough.
>
> Int.: When he's your age you think he'll be treated the same as you?
>
> L: Yea.
>
> Int.: Do you think it's important that you get the same rules at the same age?
>
> L: Yea.
>
> Int.: Why is that important?
>
> L: Umm ... I don't think it would be fair otherwise.
>
> *Leanne, aged 11*

It was clear from children's accounts that a system of transmitting rules from older to younger siblings was not only a useful system for the children involved. It also appeared that for parents the model provided a useful structure that eased the process of making appropriate decisions for their younger children and allowed them to be seen to be treating all of their children 'the same'. The children we spoke to frequently cited their parents, by words and actions, as reinforcing the model of precedence in which rules made for the eldest child in a family set the pattern for all subsequent children:

Int.:	Do you think it's fair that everyone goes to bed at different times?
D:	Yea 'cos Matt's [aged 12] old enough to stay up.
Int.:	Do you think that one day you'll be allowed to stay up late?
D:	Yea. My mother said about the same as my brother. I said, 'Mum can I go to bed the same time as Matt?' and she said when I'm the same age as him.

Dave, aged nine

Many of the children stressed the importance they placed on consistency when rules and decisions were made for themselves and their siblings; this is a key aspect of children's sense of fairness in family decision making (see Chapter 5 for further discussion on the subject of fairness):

Int.:	Is it important that you get to have the same rules as your brother and sisters had?
T:	Yea, 'cos my mum shouldn't treat any of us different.
Int.:	Do you think mum and dad always make fair decisions?
T:	Yea, they always make fair decisions.
Int.:	What do you think is fair about the decisions they make?
T:	That they are the same as my brother and sisters, they're the same as all my friends, they're nearly all allowed the same as me and my mum lets me play with friends around my house.
Int.:	Is it important that you get the same rules as your friends?
T:	It's important to me that I get the same rules as my brother and sisters.

Tom, aged 11

Most children judged the appropriateness and 'sameness' of rules and decisions in terms of children's age. It was apparent, however, that parents did not always apply rules on the basis of age alone. The children described a number of instances in which other factors had apparently influenced the differential application of rules between siblings. Kay, aged 11, for example described how her younger brother (aged nine) had different rules about where he could go because in this instance he was seen as less competent at the important skill of crossing the road:

Int.:	Does your brother have the same rules for going out to play?
K:	No, 'cos he's not allowed to go out and play on his own 'cos he's no good on roads. He can walk to school on his own and back but he's not allowed up the park.

Int.:   Was it the same when you were his age?

K: No, I was allowed up the park because I've always been better than him on the road.

Int.:   Do you think that's fair that there are different rules for you and him?

K: Yea, 'cos he's no good on the roads, like, he just doesn't look.

Other children, like 11-year-old Ellie, felt that their bad behaviour, as compared to that of their siblings, meant that they were not allowed some of the same privileges – in this case being allowed to choose her own bedtime:

Int.:   Do you think you should get to have a say in what time you go to bed?

E: Yes. Because my brother [aged 13] and sister [aged 16] got to choose theirs but I didn't.

Int.:   What time does your sister go to bed?

E: Eleven.

Int.:   What about your brother?

E: Half past ten.

Int.:   How come they get to choose their own and you don't?

E: Because in the morning I don't get up for school 'cos I don't like school. My brother and sister do, and I'm naughty for mum.

Although parents were largely seen as applying the same rules to children of the same ages (except where the circumstances or conduct of the child merited differential treatment), children also highlighted a number of instances of parents being arbitrarily inconsistent when applying rules to different children, similar to those described in Section 3.3. Children reported examples of parents either refusing to allow younger siblings the same privileges as their older siblings once they had reached the same age or of parents becoming more lenient when applying rules to younger siblings, a form of 'generational creep'. When asked whether she felt that her family made decisions in a fair way (see also Chapter 5), Gina, aged 10 said:

Some things are done in an unfair way. My big sister [aged 14] had her ears pierced when she was 13 and I had mine done when I was nine and my younger sister [aged seven] had them done when she was four or five. That's not a good way of doing it, because it's not fair on my older sister.

Children sometimes found these inconsistencies difficult to deal with, either because they felt they were simply unfair or because they disrupted the structure and predictability of age precedence. To quote 11-year-old Ellie again:

Int.:	How old do you think you have to be before you can start going places that you like?
E:	Twelve.
Int.:	Do you think 12 is a good age to make those decisions?
E:	No.
Int.:	What age do you think you should be able to make those decisions?
E:	My age now, because my brother used to go when he was 11 everywhere but I'm not allowed.
Int.:	Do you think that's fair?
E:	No, because I should be allowed.
Int.:	Why do you think it's different for you compared to your brother and sister?
E:	'Cos I don't get up in the morning and I'm always naughty. My mum told me that.
Int.:	Did you think that was fair or not fair?
E:	Not fair, because I'm the same as them.

Although the children expressed a strong wish for consistency, they were aware of and acknowledged the difficulties faced by their parents in trying to keep rules consistent while catering for the individual differences and needs that inevitably exist between siblings. In these circumstances the children reiterated the need for parents to consult their children and provide clear explanations for why rules or decision outcomes may be suitable for one child but not another.

The children also felt that consistency in making rules and decisions played an important role in helping to avoid unnecessary tension and conflict between parents and children (when they feel they have been treated unfairly) and between siblings (when they feel they have been treated unequally).

Int.:	Why is it important to have everything the same for you and your brother [aged six] and sister [aged five]?
L:	Because we'll have the same discipline, we won't always squabble about everything because we'll like the same things and not everybody will have different rules.
Int.:	Would that be a good thing or a bad thing if everybody had different rules?

> L: It would be a lot of chaos if everyone had different rules; just like the law, they keep to that and everybody abides by it.
>
> *Lauren, aged 10*

Although few children report disagreements between themselves and parents over family rules and decisions, a number did describe witnessing this type of conflict between their parents and their older siblings. Interestingly, the children did not believe that this precedent would hold for them; most do not anticipate experiencing the same types of disagreements and conflict with their parents when they are older.

> Int.:   Do you think you'll be allowed to make more decisions on your own as you get older?
>
> A: Yes, 'cos my big sister [aged 14] she makes quite a lot of decisions, but she argues quite a lot with my mum; she doesn't listen to my mum 'cos she's getting to the point where she doesn't listen any more. She makes decisions overruling my mum's decisions. I feel there are times when I'll have to make my own decision and it'll be entirely up to me.
>
> Int.:   What do you think of your big sister overruling your mum's decisions?
>
> A: I don't like it 'cos she's more bossy and my mum can't really do anything about it. If she shouts at her then my sister'll just go out somewhere.
>
> Int.:   Do you think you'll get to the stage where you overrule your mum's decisions?
>
> A: No, no, I don't think I want to get to that stage, and I don't think I will.
>
> Int.:   You don't think it just happens with being older?
>
> A: No, that was just her [the sister's] decision.
>
> *Andrew, aged 11*

4.6 Friends and other families

Overall children's accounts of family decision making make very little reference to the impact or more direct involvement of people outside their immediate family. The only real exception to this was a few children who made reference to their close friends. For these children it was apparent that friends provided a useful benchmark for assessing the appropriateness of decisions or rules that had been made for them.

> My friend is a few months younger than me. She's got an older brother
> called Sam, like 15, but she doesn't go [to town] with him; she goes with
> her friend Rosie who's about one year older than her, and she's allowed to
> go into Monruthin and Chelstow, right. But mum says I'm not allowed to
> go even with a 13-year-old, and that's three years older than me. But I'm
> not even allowed to go to the village and mum said she'll try to discuss it
> with dad, he's the main one about safety.
>
> *Lauren, aged 10*

A few children referred to rules that had been made for their friends when
judging the perceived 'fairness' of rules that had been set by their own
parents:

> Int.: Do you think it's fair, your bedtime?
>
> E: No! Because it's too early for me. All my friends get to go to
> bed at ten o'clock.
>
> Int.: Do you think it's fair, the way your mother decides where you
> can go?
>
> E: [Long pause] Not fair. 'Cos all my friends are allowed to go on
> trains and stuff but I'm not. And they go on a train to
> swimming but my mum says no.
>
> *Ellie, aged 11*

A few of the children interviewed also used their peers as a reference group when
negotiating rules or decisions with their parents, or when disputing the fairness of
some aspect of their lives:

> Int.: Why do you think she's suddenly letting you go to town on
> your own?
>
> M: I think it's 'cos all my friends do and I keep saying it's not fair
> 'cos they're going, so she's starting letting me now 'cos I'm
> getting older.
>
> Int.: Why didn't you think it was fair?
>
> M: 'Cos all my friends were going and I wasn't. And I wanted to
> start buying my own stuff.
>
> *Mandy, aged 10*

It was clear then that a number of the children we spoke to were actively observing
how their friends' families approached the process of rule and decision making. For,
although some children (11 out of 37) thought other families probably made

decisions the way their own family did, most (26 out of 37) thought others probably had different approaches to decision making.

> Most families probably do it differently 'cos we're all different, aren't we.
> *Lauren, aged 10*

Observing how decisions were made in other families also gave the children an insight into alternative ways of how family decisions could be made. Ellie, aged 11, had tried to use this as a way of changing how decisions were made in her own family, with some success:

Int.:	Do you think other families make decisions in the same way that yours does, or do you think sometimes they do it differently?
E:	Sometimes they do it differently. My friend's family, they all do it together but we don't.
Int.:	Which do you prefer?
E:	My friend's.
Int.:	Do you ever suggest that they do it like that in your family?
E:	Yea, but sometimes it works and sometimes it doesn't.

In addition, the children were able to cite what their friends' families did as examples of bad practice:

Int.:	Do you think that other families make decisions in the same way that your family does?
K:	No, because, like, my best friend Megan is allowed to go anywhere, her mum is really laid back.
Int.:	What do you think about that?
K:	Sometimes I wish my mum was a bit softer ... but I think she's [her friend's mum] is too laid back, 'cos she's always in the house and Megan is always out.
Int.:	So you wouldn't want it to be like that for you?
K:	It would be ok but I'd probably get a bit fed up ... Because I would always be out.
	Kay, aged 11

By comparison, 11-year-old Jenny stated categorically that she would have preferred her family to make decisions the way she thought other families did:

Int.:	Do you think the way your family makes decisions is the way other families make decisions?

J:	No.
Int.:	How do you think your family differs from other families?
J:	They just ... my mum and dad let me do stuff that I wanna do as long as I stay out of their hair. And the other day I said, 'Dad, will you take me to town?', 'cos I like to go to the Bear Factory, 'cos I collect teddy bears. And my dad said, 'Ok, I'll take you tomorrow. Can you wait 'til tomorrow?'. And the day after he said, 'No, I'm not taking you', and I said 'Why?' and he goes, 'I think I just said it to shut you up'.
Int.:	How do you think other families do these things?
J:	Other families might say that they couldn't go, but we could go next week, and then they'd probably go next week.
Int.:	So it's ok if it's next week provided that's what happens?
J:	Yea.

It is interesting to note that Jenny scored her family very negatively on cohesion and expressiveness and high on conflict (see Appendix 1.4.2).

Although some of the children talked about their friends, it seemed that at their current age they did not feel a noticeable amount of the 'peer pressure' that is often associated with adolescence, and to which they themselves allude. In many situations they still accepted their parents as the guiding force, as 'knowing best' and as the authority across a wide range of circumstances.

However, it was also clear that the children felt this position would change in the not-too-distant future with progress towards self-actualisation, as we have suggested. The ironic association in adolescence of independence and 'fitting-in' was beginning to be felt by some of the children in our sample. For example, when asked whether it was important where she could or could not go out to play, Jane said:

J:	Yea, because if I wanna go somewhere and I can't go, then that makes me left out with part of my social group and the next day they're going to be talking about it and I'm gonna be like, I wasn't there you know, I can't talk about it. I'd feel left out.
Int.:	Is it important to do the same as your friends?
J:	Well it's not really important but umm ... I think it's not fair because I was playing with them and then she's [mother]

taking me away from my friends to take me in, and most of the time I'd just be stuck in, and then all my friends playing out in the street and I can see them out the window. I'd feel a bit sad, a bit jealous, because they're having all the fun and I'm inside.

Jane, aged 10

Int.:	Why is it fair that you should get to decide what you wear?
J:	'Cos I'm older and I wanna look fashionable and everything and look like my friends.
Int.:	Is that important to you that you look like your friends?
J:	Yea.
Int.:	Why is that so important do you think?
J:	I'm not sure.
Int.:	How would you feel if you weren't looking fashionable and weren't looking like your friends?
J:	I wouldn't go out with my friends then.
Int.:	Why not?
J:	'Cos I'd look stupid [giggles].
Int.:	How would that make you feel?
J:	Umm, it would make me feel really annoyed and make me feel really stupid and that's about it.

Julie, aged nine

4.7 Key findings

- Children make few claims to autonomous decision making.
- Although most children want to be consulted more than they are, not all do.
- Where they do want to be consulted more is largely in relation to matters associated with developing self-identity (such as appearance or freedom of movement).
- Children do see themselves becoming more autonomous with age, according with their observations of older brothers and sisters.
- The experience of siblings is important in enabling children to understand the progressive nature of rules and domestic decision making.
- Precedents set by older siblings appear to be helpful to parents too in maintaining family rules.

- Children value consistency of decision making between different generations of the same family and between siblings, although they are sensitive to the need for differentiation on the basis of particular needs or circumstances.
- The experience of friends and other families has little bearing on patterns of decision and rule making for children at this age, except in a few cases where this conflicts with or compromises their developing sense of their own social identity.

5.   Fairness

5.1 Introduction

We have already, at several points in our account of children's understanding and experience of family decision making, made reference to ideas of 'fairness'. The importance to children of the process and outcome of family decisions being 'fair' cannot be overstated. It was apparent that children's desire for and claims to fairness operated at all levels of domestic decision making and across all domains. However, while the children's claims to fairness were expressed in straightforward terms, their understanding of what constitutes fairness in the varying contexts of family decision making was remarkably sophisticated.

5.2 Having a say

For some children, fairness in the context of decision making meant no more than being given the chance to express their views and 'having a say' (see also Section 2.3 and 4.3), to participate in decision-making processes and to be part of the 'democracy' of the family. Laura, aged 11, expressed the view shared by a number of children that being asked one's views was imperative even if it had no bearing on the outcome of a decision (in this case about where her family went on holiday):

> Int.:   Would you like to be asked where you'd like to go on holiday?
>
> L: Yea, because, umm, I like going on holiday wherever, but I would like to have a say where I would like to go, even though we won't go there. I'd like to actually say 'Well, I'd like to go to Tenerife' or 'I'd like to go to Majorca'. And even if we don't go, I don't mind then, but I would like to say.

Int.:	What's more important, that you're asked or that you get your own way?
L:	I'd like to be asked for my views.

Similarly, Leanne, supported the view that being allowed to have a say is crucial to fair decision making so that everybody is, in her terms, 'comfortable' with what is decided:

Int.:	Do you think the way that things are usually decided in your family is fair?
L:	I think it's usually fair.
Int.:	What makes it fair?
L:	That everybody gets a say in things most of the time.
Int.:	Why is that important?
L:	So that we're comfortable with the decisions we make, that everybody gets a say.
Int.:	Do you think your bedtimes were decided in a fair way?
L:	Yes.
Int.:	What made it fair?
L:	That I got a decision in it as well.
Int.:	How would you feel if you didn't get to have a decision in it?
L:	I'd feel upset because I like to have my say in things.

Leanne, aged 11

Leanne's comments illustrate the point that decisions that bear on more personal (rather than familial) matters also need to permit a degree of participation if they are to be considered 'fair'. Jo, aged 10, who is one of four children (siblings aged 7, 12 and 15), was used to different members of her family being involved in decision making depending on the issue concerned, but stressed the importance to her of being allowed to have a say in decisions which she described as *'about me'*:

Int.:	So in terms of your bedtime, do you think that the way that was done was fair?
J:	Yea, I said what time I wanted, so I think that was fair.
Int.:	Can you think what would have made it unfair?
J:	If my mum just decided and not let me say anything about it.
Int.:	Why would that be unfair?
J:	'Cos it's important I'm allowed to speak about it because it's about my bedtime.
Int.:	Do you think that it's always important that you should be able to speak about it?
J:	Yea, if it's anything to do with me.

For some children however, fairness required rather more than simply being able to express their views. While these children did not always expect to get their own way it was important that their parents took into account what they had said in a way that went beyond simply listening. Children wanted parents, where appropriate, to compromise. Jane (whose eleventh birthday is 'next week') for example, felt that her parents had made a fair decision concerning what films she was allowed to watch. Although not her preferred outcome, Jane and her parents had both compromised to reach an agreement:

J: Sometimes I'm not allowed to watch, like, certificate 18. I'm allowed most of the time to watch 15 and 12 but I'm not allowed to watch most of the films that are classified 18.

Int.:   How do you feel about that?

J: I'm happy with that, I think that's fair. Because I'm only 11 and I'm allowed to watch things that are 15, so I think that's more advantage on my behalf than on my parents. Yes, I'm happy with the good side of the bargain.

Ten-year-old Kath reiterates the idea that children and parents should be prepared to compromise over rules so that everyone 'gets a bit of what they want':

Int.:   Do you think in something like bedtimes, for example, you should have a say?

K: Yea, and I **have** had a say.

Int.:   Why's it right that you have a say?

K: Because it's not fair otherwise if my mum makes the decision.

Int.:   If you were asked, but you didn't get the bedtime you wanted, would that be fair?

K: Umm, well, like ... if my mum says, nine, and I say, half past, it's usually like quarter past so, like, we both have the time we want.

Int.:   If you disagreed, would you tell your mum or dad?

K: Umm, yea, I would tell them.

Int.:   Do you think they'd listen to what you had to say?

K: Yea, they'd listen; they'd probably change it to something that everybody liked.

Int.:   They'd try and make it that everyone agreed with it?

K: Yea, that it was fair.

Int.:   If everyone agrees, is it more fair?

K: Yea, 'cos then everybody gets a bit of what they want to have.

Having influence is not, of course, the same as having one's own way. Ten-year-old Joe, who is an only child, clearly describes a degree of mutuality and reciprocity in his relationship with his parents when it comes to deciding fairly where they will go on a family outing:

> Int.:   Do you think the way decisions are made in your family is usually fair?
>
> J: Yea, sometimes.
>
> Int.:   Give me an example of when it's fair.
>
> J: If it's fair my mother asks my father, and my father asks me, then I ask my mother. If we all got different decisions, I ask my mother what she wants to do and then I ask my father what he wants to do and then I join them together. I don't think about myself, and I think of somewhere where we can all go, [somewhere that's] nice, and then we go there.

That we spoke earlier of Joe having generally poor communications with his parents (Section 4.3), whereas now we are describing their relationship in terms of reciprocity and mutuality, highlights the complexities inherent in family decision making. Joe's apparently contradictory description of his relationship with his parents provide a good foil for Lee's descriptions. For Lee, despite enjoying a very good all-round rapport with his parents (see for example Section 2.2, 4.3), he nonetheless described how he was excluded from the important matter of his attending his aunt's funeral.

Most children, like Joe, are actively concerned that family decisions should be made by a clearly defined, fair process, rather than that they simply get what they want:

> Int.:   Do you think that the way things are decided in your family is usually done in a fair way?
>
> E: Yea.
>
> Int.:   What is it about it that makes it fair?
>
> E: Everybody has a say about what they want to do even if we don't get to do it.
>
> *Ellen, aged nine*

If the decision or rule-making process was deemed to be fair, most children (including 10-year-old Lee) felt that the outcome was, for all concerned, at least:

> ... a bit fair ...

This usually meant either that in the immediate term, to quote 10-year-old Kath:

... there was something for everyone ...

Or in the longer term that others would, as Zara, aged nine, explained:

... get their turn [to choose] ...

Provided, as nine-year-old Ellen put it:

... it was done in a fair way ...

Most children were willing to accept that, even if it was not what they wanted, the outcome was nonetheless fair.

> Int.: Can you give me an example of something that you think is unfair?
>
> L: Umm ... yea ... when we went to McArthur Glen I thought that was unfair and I did say something, but I got a row.
>
> Int.: Did you think it was unfair because they hadn't asked you about it, or did you think it was unfair because they were going to McArthur Glen and you didn't want to go?
>
> L: Because they didn't ask me, because they know that I wanted to go out so that's probably why they thought 'Oh, we'll just go to McArthur Glen'.
>
> Int.: If they said, 'We want to go to McArthur Glen, what do you think about it?' If you said you didn't really want to go and they said 'Well, we understand that you don't want to go but we're going to go anyway', do you think that would be fair?
>
> L: Yea, because they would have asked me first not just gone.
>
> Int.: That's the important thing?
>
> L: Yea.
>
> *Lee, aged 10*

Children's desire to ensure a fair outcome by means of a fair (inclusive) process was echoed in their comments on the means used in their own families to resolve whole-family issues. As we have indicated (Section 2.2), voting was one of the most common strategies used in such circumstances. Kylie, aged 11, describes how voting is sometimes used in her family to decide what they will have to eat. In this system Kylie considers it fair that the majority vote wins:

> K: My mum won't cook all different meals. If we all want different then we'll have a vote and which one's the highest gets it.
>
> Int.: Is that a system that works well in your family?

K:	Yea. It works well because then we all know it's fair and we agree.
Int.:	Why is it fair?
K:	Because we all get a say, and like if it was three against one then the majority of them want it so we should have it.
Int.:	What if you're the one?
K:	I wouldn't mind 'cos everyone else should have what they want whether I like it or not.

John, aged 10, who has two elder siblings aged 17 and 18, described how they often have difficulty in his family finding things to do that suit everyone. As a consequence his family had tried a range of strategies to try and reach family agreement. Here for example, he describes how they choose where to go on holiday by randomly picking a piece of paper. This was deemed fair because everybody was given an equal chance to get what he or she wanted:

Int.:	What if you all had different opinions, how would you decide?
J:	Different ways really. Once we hold [sic] things in a hat when we were [sic] going on holiday, pieces of paper and chucked them all on the floor and picked one.
Int.:	If your suggestion doesn't get picked is that fair?
J:	Yea.
Int.:	Why's it fair?
J:	Because if I can't go, it's just tough, ain't it, I just can't go.
Int.:	What's the important bit? Is it important that you discuss it or is it important that you get your way?
J:	It's important that we discuss.
Int.:	Is that better than getting your way?
J:	Yea.

A similar system was used in Gina's family to determine what they would have for tea:

Int.:	How do you decide normally what you're going to have to eat?
G:	Me and my little sister usually talk in the morning about it and say what we want. We're not allowed beef but we can have Quorn meat that's made with vegetables. But say my [older] brother and sister aren't home, we can choose.
Int.:	Do you and your little sister normally agree about what you want?
G:	No, we put what we want in a hat and choose.
Int.:	Is that a good system?

G: Yea, 'cos she doesn't mind if I win and I don't really care if she wins.

Int.:   How would you feel if she won every time?

G: No, because it's fair. It's a 50:50 chance.

Gina, aged 10

Where turn-taking was the preferred means of resolving whole-family issues, children like Ruhana and Dave were clearly used to having to wait but were happy to do so because they trusted that they would get their turn in due course:

Int.:   What if you all want different things?

R: My mum would say, like, if it was my birthday then my mum would say I'd get to choose and then my family would have to go along with me and all that, 'cos when it's their birthdays they get to go where they want and I go along with them.

Int.:   Is that a fair way to do it?

R: Yes.

Int.:   Do you think the way your family make decisions is usually fair?

R: Yes.

Int.:   Why is it fair?

R: Because when some of us want to go to the beach and some of us want to have a McDonald's, we have it in turns and I think that's fair because all of us get to do whatever we want. And like it goes from smallest to biggest [youngest to eldest child] so I'm the last one to choose, and I have to agree with them and then they have to agree with me.

Ruhana, aged 10

Int.:   If you wanted to go to America and your brother and sisters decided they wanted to go somewhere else and they got to go to their place, what would you think about that?

D: Ok, 'cos it's still a holiday to me.

Int.:   Do you think that's fair?

D: Yea, I think it alright 'cos sometimes I get to go to the places I want, sometimes my brother wants to go to a place he wants and we go the place he wants.

Dave, aged nine

For a small number of children however, 'fairness' was dependent on whether they got their own way:

Int.:   So it's just the going out with your friends which is sometimes unfair? What's unfair about that?

K: If I'm not allowed to go out I just get really bored.

Int.:   So if they asked you what you wanted, if you then didn't get your own way, would that be fair?

K: Probably not.

Int.:   So you think that fairness is about getting what you want?

K: Yea.

Kay, aged 11

Int.:   The fact that your dad asks everybody in the family what they want, is that important?

E: Yea.

Int.:   Does that make it fair?

E: Yea.

Int.:   So what if you all get to have a say but then you don't get to go where you want, is that fair?

E: No, 'cos I like going places where I wanna go.

Ellie, aged 11

5.3 Equity

We have seen already (see Section 4.5) that children expect, to some degree, consistency of decision making across the generations of their brothers and sisters. Equity of treatment between siblings was clearly important to many children's idea of fairness:

Int.:   Is it important that things are fair?

J: Well I think it's a little bit important because things like, say there were a few sweets left over from a party or something and I ate all the sweets, it'd be quite sad on my brother, but if my brother had them it would be unfair on me.

Int.:   Is it important that it's fair between you and your brother?

J: Yea.

Jill, aged nine

Children's need for equitable (and therefore 'fair') treatment was apparently as much for their siblings' benefit as for their own:

Int.:	Why did they just ask you and not sister [aged seven]?
L:	Because it was a bit easier for me to make the decision than her but then the next time, when it was easier for her to make the decision, they would have asked her and not me.
Int.:	Why do you think it was easier for you to make that decision?
L:	I don't know why; perhaps it was because I was easy to go with.
Int.:	Do you think that it would be fair to ask just the eldest child?
L:	No, because you all need to get involved, not just one of you or two but all of the family.

Lee, aged 10

Children's sense of fairness among brothers and sisters does not always imply that each is treated identically. Children suggested that decisions should be determined by context and consider the need of individuals at any given time:

Int.:	Is part of what you're saying that your little sister goes later to bed than you did when you were her age?
A:	Yea, mainly because she gets more scared than I did. She's a lot more scared of the dark and everything.
Int.:	So, she stays up until someone else is going to bed?
A:	Yea.
Int.:	Is it unfair that you're little sister gets to stay up later than you did when you were small?
A:	I don't really think so because when I was small I wasn't actually scared. She's actually scared so it's unfair if somebody had to go being scared. And, she'd have nightmares and scream and wake everyone up.

Andrew, aged 11

That fairness is determined by context is clearly illustrated by Natasha, aged nine, who felt that fairness sometimes meant being excluded when the issues were private to her parents:

Int.:	Do you think that the decisions that are made in your family are fair?
N:	Yep.
Int.:	What's fair about them?
N:	They always make sure we're involved. But if it's something private, like this [taking part in our study], confidential, then they'll say, sorry, but they wouldn't make it obvious that they're hiding something.

Int.:	So your parents might keep some things just to themselves? And what do you think about that?
N:	I think that's fair enough, 'cos, like, it is fair, they're grown-ups and it might be a bit private, so that's fair.

What became clear from our interviews with children, however, was that children's claims on fairness were not always fully appreciated or understood by their parents, especially where these were explicitly linked to a child's increasing sense of and desire for a greater degree of autonomy. As a result, rules or decisions that parents seemed to believe to be fair were not always seen as such by their children:

Int.:	Do you think that it's fair if everyone gets a say?
J:	Yes I do, definitely.
Int.:	What happens then if everyone has a different opinion?
J:	I think my mother should adapt to my opinion more and not just about her opinion.
Int.:	Does that mean actually letting you have your way?
J:	No, my mum should agree with me more often. Just agree with me.
Int.:	Does she explain why she is not agreeing with you?
J:	No [firmly].
Int.:	Would you like her to?
J:	If she says something like, 'No, you're not allowed' I would like her to say why I am not allowed to go to this place instead of, 'No, you're not allowed'. If she said something like 'No, you're not allowed because I am working tonight', or 'No, because I want you to watch the baby for 10 minutes 'till I go down the shop', I wouldn't mind then because then I would have a reason not to go. If I haven't got a reason then there is no point in me not going.
Int.:	Have you ever asked why?
J:	Sometimes I do.
Int.:	How do you feel when you do that?
J:	I feel like I'm defending what I'm saying. Sometimes I feel I have to defend myself 'cos sometimes she doesn't [agree] … well, most of the time she agrees with me.
Int.:	Do you think it will change?

J: I don't think so because she is 36 years old now, and she has been like this for 36 years and in another 36 years she'll probably still be like it.

Jane, aged 10

5.4 Key findings

- Children make sophisticated moral judgements on the quality of decision making in their families which they express in the language of fairness.
- Children incline very strongly to the practice of participatory decision making predicated on their sense of fairness.
- Fairness is a differentiated concept; it has more to do with being treated equitably than being treated identically, especially in relation to brothers and sisters.
- Fairness is a function of the process of decision making, not the outcome.
- Fairness is applied by children as a 'moral lever' in seeking to negotiate compromises with parents.
- Children do recognise the limits of fairness and will, for example, regard some matters as 'private' between their parents.
- Parents do not always recognise the importance of fairness to children.

6. Conclusions and reflections

6.1 Introduction

In this chapter, we begin by synthesising our key findings and providing a general account of the processes of family decision making. We then consider the implications of our findings, particularly as these relate to children whose experience of family life is disrupted or where family life is otherwise in transition. We also consider the relevance of children's sense of fairness to extra-familial contexts in which their participation is invited.

6.2 Family decision making

We have suggested (in Section 2.1) that the internal life of families can be understood as an instance of a complex system. Its fundamental constituents are individual family members and their temperaments, capacities, attitudes and beliefs. These individuals form a series of relationships. Some of these are formed around function (parent–child, parent–parent) but such relationships may cross both age and gender boundaries (mother–son, for example) (see Pryor and Rodgers, 2001: 46–7). Each of these sub-systems interacts with the others, and the whole of a family's interactions and relationships may be said to be greater than the sum of its parts, in that each also feeds into defining the particular micro-culture of the family.

Evidence for this view can be found in research into the effects of intra-family processes that has increasingly recognised whole-family functioning as an important indirect variable on developmental outcomes for children (see Johnson 2001; Borinne and others 1991). More recently, resilience has also been identified as a quality of families as well as an attribute of some individuals within it (Patterson and Fisher 2002).

Our research would suggest that the processes whereby this complexity is managed, at least as far as everyday decision making in families is concerned, are equally complex, subtle and diffuse. We found few examples of explicit or formal means of decision making or of negotiation over the application of family rules. Rather, our findings demonstrate decision making to be a largely **implicit** process that relies to a considerable degree on a cumulative, shared understanding of the family's particular history, traditions and routine ways of transacting its affairs. For example, both children and parents typically rely more on indirect or disguised forms of negotiation (such as 'being good') over points of difference than on formal, essentially verbal means of negotiation. Precedent, particularly sibling precedent, is an important guide for children to the direction of their development and is an aid to consistency and predictability in decision making for both children and parents.

Generally, children express confidence in the unarticulated structures and processes of family decision making and in the capacity of their parents to make 'good decisions' (ones that are well-informed and inclusive). This confidence may be born of familiarity, intimate knowledge and the trust that develops through habit and custom. Children concede authority to their parents in most instances, and rarely question their parents' protective, nurturing orientation towards them. It may be that children perceive an equivalence in terms of the distribution of parental authority and commitment, even if their conversations with us indicated a more uneven distribution of parental engagement in the tasks of parenting, largely along gendered lines. In a sense, this apparent contradiction may be indicative of the degree to which children's faith in their parents' capacity to co-parent survives any direct observation of their practice.

Children's trust in their parents is not an uncritical or unreasoned one however, and relies on parents being able to demonstrate their competence to make 'good decisions'. This requires family decision making to be flexible and responsive, especially to children's developing sense of agency and their progress towards independence and autonomy. We should add that we noted substantial variation in children's progress towards self-actualisation (and in their confidence to make competent decisions), which may serve as a brake on any dogmatic application of 'developmentalism'. This also demonstrates that not only are children's own experiences differentiated within a narrow age range, but also that families are adaptable to the pace set and required by children. Most children recognised that progress towards more autonomy and developing a greater capacity to make decisions was an incremental, learning process.

Clearly therefore, intra-family processes are to be understood as **dynamic**: as responding to the forces which bear on them. In this study, we have not considered in any detail, the meso-, exo- or macro-systems (Bronfenbrenner 1979) with which families engage. We are aware that ecological perspectives on family life (see Hetherington and Stanley-Hagan 2002) can usefully extend the family-systems framework that we are applying and reflect how the internal life of families is influenced by the social ecology (socio-economic status, environmental resources and the like) in which they are located. Indeed, our study has suggested that, from the child's perspective, neither other families, including those of their friends, nor wider external forces bear very directly on the patterns and outcomes of decision making in families.

The dynamic nature of family life is reflected, however, in the degree to which children are able to exercise their claim to participate in the everyday routines of domestic decision making. The children in our study incline very strongly to inclusive decision making. Given the relative powerlessness of children – both generally, as citizens, and specifically as members of a family where, by common consent, parents have the ultimate authority – it is important to recognise the importance that children's claims to 'fairness' have in the context of the limited forms of democracy practiced by families. Claims to fairness may be the most effective 'moral lever' that children can use to influence the management of the family's affairs.

It should be recognised that fairness is a function of the process of decision making, not the outcome. We note also that fairness, for most children, is divorced from ideas of selfishness (of getting one's own way) and that it can be applied to serve the interests of all family members, possibly even protecting younger brothers and sisters, as well as themselves. As such, the moral claim to fairness can be set against the child's relative incompetence and incapacity to make and apply decisions for him or herself. Once accepted within the family, the moral imperative to act fairly is vital to a child's progress towards autonomy and self-actualisation in so far as it permits the child to be included, listened to and have some influence over his or her life at home. Without the space for engagement that claims to fairness open up, a child's progress towards independence might prove much more conflictual. This realisation may explain some of the emotional power that children often invest in their sense of what is or is not fair, something that may not always be recognised by parents, although its potential to contribute to consistency of parenting is self-evident.

Family decision making is complex, implicit and subtle, founded on confidence, intimate knowledge and trust. This trust, however, is open to question, and the process requires a degree of inclusiveness and participation, and is one over which children make sophisticated moral judgements. To characterise it in this way is to recognise it as a dynamic, adaptable and differentiated set of processes and beliefs in which children are, to varying degrees, active and 'apprentice' participants. When children and families face challenges or major disruptions to their lives together, the integrity and effectiveness of the process we have described may be compromised.

6.3 Implications

We do not intend, however, to locate our findings entirely in the context of 'clinical' populations or to relate them only to those families in transition. Our findings should resonate strongly with 'ordinary' families in unexceptional circumstances. The determinants of effective parenting have been widely debated elsewhere and have included discussion of the nature of parent–child relationships (Pryor and Rodgers 2001: 252), parenting style and beliefs (Baumrind 1967, 1971, 1991; Bornstein 1991), the degree and type of parental involvement (Loeber and Stouthamer-Loeber 1986) and the nature of the parent–parent relationship (Erel and Burman 1995), for example. We regard our findings as contributing to the recognition that **being** a parent is more than **doing** as a parent. Being a parent, like being a family, is an osmotic process, nuanced and adaptive. It is an evolutionary process that may be skill-based but which is not reducible simply to a set of skills. It also requires trust, access to a shared history, an attitude of inclusiveness, fairness and flexibility.

The simple recognition of the complexity of everyday familial decision making, and so, by inference, the complexity of family life and of parenting in particular, runs counter to strong currents in evidence within certain professional groups with an interest in families. For example, one of the Department for Education and Skills/Department of Health's most recent publications, *Supporting Parents* (Quinton 2004), which is an overview of 'messages from research', tends to a very instrumental appreciation of what it means to parent. While acknowledging, but not elaborating, that parenting is also a 'key social relationship' (p. 26), it repeatedly makes reference to parenting **tasks**, approvingly citing Pugh and others' (1994) formulation of parenting before commenting that (p. 27):

> Difficulty in meeting these aims does not mean that there is something missing in parents' capacity to do the job. Most of us as parents are usually good at some of the things and less good at others. Parenting is something that parents **do**, not something that parents **have**. (Original emphasis.)

Our findings would argue for a more sophisticated understanding of parenting within the experiential context of a family.

Quinton's comments are of a piece however with a tendency in social work and elsewhere towards more instrumental, managerialist and 'rational-technical' responses to complex social situations and conditions. It is such responses that have reduced some areas of social work practice to no more than ticking boxes (see Butler and Pugh 2004). Such abstracted forms of practice in turn have been described as part of a wider attempt 'to rationalise and scientise increasing areas of social work activity with the introduction of ever-more-complex procedures and systems of audit – whereby it is assumed that the world can be subjected to prediction and calculation' (Jordan and Parton 2004: 31).

Our findings would tend to support Jordan and Parton's interest in rediscovering, embracing and working with the inherent complexity of life within families and within society more generally. Trevillion (2000: 511), regards social work itself as 'an inherently complex activity', balancing its 'dual allegiance to both welfare structures (modernism) and individual agency and creativity (postmodernism)' and we would suggest that this is necessarily so if it is to respond effectively in those circumstances where children and families need help or at times of transition. For a substantial number of families, such transitions may include divorce, non-elective single parenthood (perhaps through the death or desertion of a partner) and the making of step-families.

Most of the children in our sample were living with both of their birth parents and our findings do not allow us to speculate very far on how the complex process of decision making may vary within single parent families. While other research does not present a settled account of the processes and outcomes for children of being brought up in a single parent household, it does seem likely to us that the demands of managing the complex process that we have identified may produce stress for both children and their parents, in addition to that experienced by many single parents as a result of reduced socio-economic status and opportunities, reduced opportunities for instrumental and emotional support, or any other stresses consequent upon the process of family break-up.

Similarly, there would seem to be considerable potential for confusion and conflict where settled and un-interrogated ways of going about managing everyday life are interrupted. Such interruptions occur when families break up and new ones are formed. In the case of 'blended' families (such as step-families or foster families), conflict and confusion seem to us more likely than not if one considers that such families cannot rely on precedent or a commonly held stock of experience of how the family 'does things'. In blended families, previous family micro-cultures may be significantly different (we noted considerable variation between families over the form and nature of their 'democracy' for example) and children and parents may be at differing stages on the route to autonomous decision making. In the case of step-families in particular, where the adults are working out how to co-parent without the shared experience of having learned how to parent together, and where children are faced with accepting the authority of someone whom they are, at this point, unable to trust to the degree that they have trusted a now-absent parent, and where none of the parties are likely to have any experience of more explicit structures for making routine family decisions, it is not surprising to find evidence of difficulties in fully 'blending'. Many other factors will contribute to the challenges faced by step-families, of course (see Pryor and Rodgers, 2001: 186 ff.), including the relationship history of the adults, the stability of the new arrangements, and additional environmental stressors (such as the formal processes of divorce). Nonetheless, it seems to us that the patient fashioning of the 'new' family's way of managing its everyday business to the point where this becomes once more implicit and accepted without much question or regard is a particularly stiff test for all of those involved.

In the case of children separated from their parents through entering into public care or through extended illness, for example, it has been widely recognised that losing the thread of the family history is detrimental to their longer-term welfare (see Bullock and others, 1993: 16f.). Our findings would support this position and may take us further towards understanding some of the adjustment difficulties that children will face when entering out-of-family placements. In cases of substitute family care in particular, the difficulties described above in relation to step-families will be experienced by the child rather more than the host family, especially as the child may not have developed the tools and personal skills for the more explicit negotiation of family rules in his or her birth family. Such difficulties will be compounded where a child is subject to multiple moves. Finding out how a family makes its decisions and formulates its rules is not the work of a moment or even of a couple of weeks or months.

Finally, in turning to extra-familial contexts, we would draw attention to the symbolic as well as the actual force of children's claims to fairness. In the context of their relative powerlessness, fair process (if not a fair outcome) is important to children and should be understood as a legitimate moral claim on the actions of adults, especially where adults seek to engage children in formal participatory processes, such as school councils.

We do not presume to make recommendations to either parents or professionals although it seems to us as though certain principles emerge naturally from our reflections upon our findings. It is important for all of those with an interest in families and in the provision of services to families to:

- understand and respect the complexity of family processes, family histories and the particular ways that families have of going about their everyday business
- understand and respect the diversity of family micro-cultures, and resist the impetus to categorise or to abstract behaviours and relationships from their context
- respect the authority of parents, the confidence that many children have in their parents and the capacity of children to engage meaningfully and purposefully in determining the conduct of family life
- respect children's inclination towards participatory forms of engagement in family life and be sensitive to children who are in the process of developing their capacity for autonomy and independence
- respect and respond to children's claims to fairness and equitable treatment.

References

Alanen, L 'Gender and generation: Feminism and the "child question"', in Quartrup, J and others (eds) (1994) *Childhood matters: Social theory, practice and politics.* Aldershot: Avebury.

Bar-Yam, Y (2003) *Dynamics of complex systems.* Boulder, Colo.: Westview Press.

Baumrind, D (1967) 'Child care practices anteceding three patterns of preschool behaviour', *Genetic Psychology Monographs,* 75, 43–83.

Baumrind, D (1971) 'Current patterns of parental authority', *Developmental Psychology Monographs,* 4, 1, part 2.

Baumrind, D 'Effective parenting during early adolescent transition', in Cowan, P and Hetherington, E (eds) (1991) *Family transitions.* Mahwah, N.J.: Lawrence Erlbaum.

Borrine, M and others (1991) 'Family conflict and adolescent adjustment in intact, divorced, and blended families', *Journal of Consulting and Clinical Psychology,* 59, 5, 753–5.

Bornstein, M (1991) *Cultural approaches to parenting.* Hillsdale, N.J.: Lawrence Erlbaum.

Bronfenbrenner, U (1979) *The ecology of human development.* Cambridge, Mass.: Harvard University Press.

Buchner, P, Bois-Reymond, M and Kruger, H 'Growing up in three European regions', in Chisholm, L (ed) (1995) *Growing up in Europe: Contemporary horizons in childhood and youth studies.* Berlin: de Gruyter.

Bullock, R, Little, M and Milham, S (1993) *Residential care for children - a review of the research.* London: HMSO.

Butler, I and Pugh, R 'The politics of social work research', in Lovelock, R, Lyons, K and Powell, J (eds) (2004) *Reflecting on social work: Discipline and profession.* Aldershot: Ashgate.

Butler, I and others (2003) *Divorcing children: Children's experience of their parents' divorce.* London: Jessica Kingsley.

Butler, I and Williamson, H (1994) *Children speak: Children, trauma and social work.* London: Longman/NSPCC.

Department of Health, (2000) *Framework for the assessment of children in need.* London: Stationery Office.

Erel, O and Burman, B (1995) 'Interrelatedness of marital relations and parent–child relations: A meta-analytic review', *Psychological Bulletin*, 118, 1, 108–32.

Giddens, A (1992) *The transformation of intimacy: Sexuality, love and eroticism in modern societies.* Oxford: Polity.

Harter, S (1985) *Manual for the self-perception profile for children.* Denver, Colo.: University of Colorado.

Hetherington, E and Stanley-Hagan, M 'Parenting in divorced and remarried families', in Bornstein, M (ed) (2002) *Handbook of parenting. Vol. 3: Being and becoming a parent.* Mahwah, N.J.: Lawrence Erlbaum.

James, A and Prout, A 'A new paradigm for the sociology of childhood? Provenance, promise and problems', in James, A and Prout, A (eds) (1991) *Constructing and reconstructing childhood: Contemporary issues in the sociological study of childhood.* London: Falmer.

James, A and James, A (2004) *Childhood: Theory, policy and practice.* Basingstoke: Palgrave Macmillan.

Johnson, V (2001) 'Marital interaction, family organisation and differences in parenting behaviour: Explaining variations across family interaction contexts', *Family Processes*, 40, 3, 333–42.

Jordan, B and Parton, N 'Social work, the public sphere and civil society' in Lovelock, R, Lyons, K and Powell, J (eds) (2004) *Reflecting on social work: Discipline and profession.* Aldershot: Ashgate.

Loeber, R and Stouthamer-Loeber, M 'Family factors as correlates and predictors of juvenile conduct problems and delinquency', in Tory, M and Morris, N (1986) (eds) *Crime and justice (Vol. 7).* Chicago: University of Chicago Press.

Moos, RH and Moos, BS (1981) *The family environment scale manual.* Palo Alto, Calif.: Consulting Psychologists Press.

Neale, B (2002) 'Dialogues with children: Participation and choice in family decision-making', *Childhood*, 9, 4, 456–75.

Patterson, G and Fisher, P 'Recent developments in our understanding of parenting: Bidirectional effects, causal models and the search for parsimony', in Bornstein, M (ed) (2002) *Handbook of parenting. Vol. 5: Practical issues in parenting.* Mahwah, N.J.: Lawrence Erlbaum.

Pryor, J and Rodgers, B (2001) *Children in changing families: Understanding children's worlds.* Oxford: Blackwell.

Pugh. G, De'Ath, E and Smith, C (1994) *Confident parents, confident children: Policy and practice in parent education and support.* London: National Children's Bureau.

Quartrup, J (1994) 'Recent developments in research and thinking on childhood', paper delivered at the XXXI *International Sociological Association Committee on Family Research*, London: 28–30 April.

Quinton, D (2004) *Supporting parents: Messages from research.* London: Jessica Kingsley.

Robinson, M and others 'Children's experience of their parents' divorce', in Jensen, A-M and McKee, L (eds) (2003) *Children and the changing family.* London: Routledge Falmer.

Robinson, M, Scanlan, L and Butler, I 'It feels normal that other people are split up but not **your** mum and dad: Divorce through the eyes of children', in Bentley, G and Mace, R (eds) (forthcoming) *Alloparenting in human societies*, Cambridge, UK: Cambridge University Press.

Trevillion, S (2000) 'Social work, social networks and network knowledge', *British Journal of Social Work*, 30, 505–17.

Wintersberger, H 'The ambivalence of modern childhood: A plea for a European strategy for children', in Wintersberger, H (ed) (1996) *Children on the way from marginality towards citizenship. Childhood policies: Conceptual and practical issues*. Vienna: European Centre for Social Welfare Policy and Research.

Appendix 1: Research methods and process

As part of their design and development Phase 1 and Phase 2 methods were piloted with children in the eight to 11 age range.

A1.1 Phase 1 quick-think task

The quick-think task involved children working as a group to compile a list of decisions families might make. The task was initiated by asking children to think of a normal day or week in their own lives and the decisions that might arise. As well as providing valuable data, the task was designed as a warm-up activity for the children.

A1.2 Phase 1 family vignettes

Each vignette presented a different scenario and had a set of questions to prompt discussion. In addition to the original scenario, each vignette had several alternative versions. These were created by systematically changing variables within the original scenario while holding the overall family situation constant. Varying each vignette systematically was designed to produce comparative data with which to explore whether and/or how decision making is affected by changes in situational and individual characteristics.

In each group session, the children were given a copy of a vignette (without the prompt questions, see Section A1.3). The researcher read through the scenario with the children before opening up the discussion. The original scenario and its alternative versions were discussed before moving on to the next vignette. Each group discussed all three vignettes. The order in which they were presented to groups was randomised to control for order bias in the data. The vignettes were completed after the quick-think task.

The vignettes were developed to stimulate discussion. We are aware that, as a method, vignettes risk constraining discussion and/or directing participants' thoughts. In fact, however, they succeeded in stimulating open, wide-ranging discussion, including spontaneous accounts of children's own experience of decision making. Analysis shows that children found the scenarios meaningful in terms of their own lives. Children frequently moved from describing how vignette characters thought, felt and behaved, to explaining how they, or family members, thought, felt or behaved. They also often moved spontaneously from the vignette scenario to recount events from their own family life.

A1.3 Family vignettes

Joe's family

Joe is nine years old. Joe lives with his mum and dad, his sister Kate who is six years old and his brother Dan who is 14 years old.

Joe's dad has been offered a new job in Australia.

It has been decided that the family will move to live in Australia.

Interviewer's Questions
- Who do you think decided that Joe's family would move to Australia?
- Do you think Joe helped make the decision?
- How do you think Joe feels about how the decision was made?
- Do you think that Joe should have helped make the decision?
- Why?

Now think about Joe's brother and sister.
- Do you think they helped make the decision about going to Australia?
- Do you think that they should have helped make the decision?
- Why?
- If Joe's family were moving to the next town, would it be the same?

Alice's family

Alice is 10 years old. Alice lives with her mum and dad, her brother Tom who is seven years old and her sister Louise who is 15 years old.

Alice's family have gone to the supermarket on the way home from school to buy something for their tea.

It has been decided that they will have pizza and salad.

Interviewer's Questions

- Who do you think decided what Alice's family would have for their tea?
- Do you think Alice helped make the decision?
- How does Alice feel about how the decision was made?
- Do you think Alice should have helped make the decision?
- Why?

Now think about Alice's brother and sister.

- Do you think they helped make the decision about what they had for tea?
- Do you think they should have helped make the decision?
- Why?
- If Alice's family were going out for tea instead would it be the same?

Molly's family

Molly is nine years old. Molly lives with her mum and dad, her brother Jake who is also nine years old and her sister Anna who is 14 years old.

Molly's family are all going bowling together.

It has been decided that Molly will wear her new jeans and new t-shirt.

Interviewer's Questions

- Who do you think decided what Molly was going to wear?
- Do you think Molly helped make the decision?
- How do you think Molly feels about how the decision was made?
- Do you think Molly should have helped make the decision?
- Why?

Now think about Molly's brother and sister.

- Do you think they decided what her brother/sister were going to wear?
- Do you think her brother/sister should have helped make the decision?
- Why?
- If Molly was going out with her friend instead of her family, would it be the same?

A1.4 Phase 2 interview schedule (qualitative data)

Pilot work indicated that the interview schedule was a useful means of stimulating wide-ranging discussion. Moreover, children did not feel constrained to discuss only the topics and themes suggested by the interview; they introduced other topics, and raised other issues.

A1.5 Phase 2 Activity Book (quantitative data)

Children provided demographic information and completed measures assessing self-worth, family functioning, and child–parent communication and child involvement. These data were collected by means of an Activity Book designed for the purpose.

A1.5.1 Demographic information and self-worth (See Table 1)

Table 1 provides a summary of the demographic and self-worth (Harter 1985) data collected in Phase 2. Across these variables there were no statistically significant differences between children in any of the four Phase 2 schools, other than in terms of ethnicity. As confirmed by Welsh Assembly Census data, only the city school had pupils from ethnic minority groups. Ethnicity, however, was not significantly associated with any other of the variables assessed by the Activity Book.

A1.5.2 Family functioning (See Table 2)

The Family Relationship Index (Moos and Moos 1981) was developed for use with adolescents and adults. It comprises 27 items assessing three subscales (see below). After pilot work, we reduced the original 27 items to 12 (four per subscale),

Table 1: Phase 2: Child and family variables and child self-worth

Child and family variables	Full study sample 48 children	Post-industrial urban school 12 children	New town urban school 12 children	Rural school 12 children	City school 12 children
Average age[1]	10 (0.9)	9.8 (0.8)	9.8 (0.9)	9.8 (1.0)	10.5 (0.6)
Range	8–11	9–11	8–11	8–11	10–11
Girls	30, 62.5%	6, 50.0%	7, 58.3%	7, 58.3%	10, 83.3%
Boys	18, 37.5%	6, 50.0%	5, 41.7%	5, 41.7%	2, 16.7%
White-British	43, 89.6%	12, 100.0%	12, 100.0%	12, 100.0%	7, 58.3%
Black/Ethnic Minority	5, 10.4%	–	–	–	5, 41.7%
Average number of siblings[1]	1.9 (1.2)	1.3 (0.9)	2.0 (1.2)	2.0 (0.9)	2.4 (1.5)
Range	0–6	0–3	1–5	1–3	1–6
Sibling age range (in years)	1–24	1–16	1–19	1–19	6–24
Parents child lives with:					
Mother and father	44, 91.7%	12, 100.0%	12, 100.0%	10, 83.3%	10, 83.3%
Mother only	2, 4.2%	–	–	1, 8.3%	1, 8.3%
Mother and boyfriend	2, 4.2%	–	–	1, 8.3%	1, 8.3%
Family socio-economic classification:[2]					
Managerial and professional	7, 14.6%	1, 8.3%	–	4, 33.3%	2, 16.7%
Intermediate occupations	10, 20.8%	3, 25.0%	–	5, 41.7%	2, 16.7%
Routine and manual occupations	25, 52.1%	7, 58.3%	10, 83.3%	3, 25.0%	5, 41.7%
Unemployed	6, 12.5%	1, 8.3%	2, 16.7%	–	3, 25.0%
Child's Average Self-Worth Score[3]	3.2 (0.6)	3.1 (0.5)	3.1 (0.8)	3.3 (0.5)	3.2 (0.7)
Scoring Range	1.5–4.0	2.0–3.8	1.5–4.0	2.0–4.0	2.0–4.0

1. Figures in brackets are standard deviations.
2. Coded using father's occupation or, if father unemployed or 'absent', on mother's occupation. Coded using The National Statistics Socio-Economic Classification, 2001, available at www.statistics.gov.uk/methods_quality/ns_sec/ (Accessed on 15 April 2005).
3. The Self-Perception Profile for Children (Harter 1985) assesses children's sense of self-worth. The scoring range is 1 (least adequate) to 4 (most adequate). Self-worth is defined as 'the extent to which child likes him/herself as a person/is happy with way (s)he leads his or her life/is generally happy with self as a person'.

Table 2: Family functioning

Subscale	Full study sample 48 children	Post-industrial urban school 12 children	New town urban school 12 children	Rural school 12 children	City school 12 children
Cohesion					
4 low cohesion	–	–	–	–	–
5	3, 6.3%	1, 8.3%	–	–	2, 16.7%
6 mid point	2, 4.2%	1, 8.3%	1, 8.3%	–	–
7	16, 33.3%	6, 50.0%	4, 33.3%	3, 25.0%	3, 25.0%
8 high cohesion	27, 56.3%	4, 33.3%	7, 58.3%	9, 75.0%	7, 58.3%
Expressiveness					
4 low expressiveness	4, 8.3%	–	1, 8.3%	2, 16.7%	1, 8.3%
5	10, 20.8%	1, 8.3%	2, 16.7%	3, 25.0%	4, 33.3%
6 mid point	14, 29.2%	5, 41.7%	3, 25.0%	3, 25.0%	3, 25.0%
7	19, 39.6%	5, 41.7%	6, 50.0%	4, 33.3%	4, 33.3%
8 high expressiveness	1, 2.1%	1, 8.3%	–	–	–
Conflict					
4 high conflict	–	–	–	–	–
5	17, 35.4%	3, 25.0%	4, 33.3%	5, 41.7%	5, 41.7%
6 mid point	14, 29.2%	3, 25.0%	4, 33.3%	4, 33.3%	3, 25.0%
7	17, 35.4%	6, 50.0%	4, 33.3%	3, 25.0%	4, 33.3%
8 low conflict	–	–	–	–	–

retaining only items that the pilot children found comprehensible and meaningful. This modification allowed us to administer our version of the index to the pre-adolescent children (aged eight to 11) who took part in our study. Correlations run on the Phase 2 data indicate that the items we retained have a subscale structure and valence consistent with those of the original 27-item Family Relationship Index.

The subscales measured are defined as:

- Cohesion: commitment, help and support that family members provide each other.
- Expressiveness: tendency to act openly and express feelings directly.
- Conflict: openly expressed anger, aggression, conflict.

The scoring range for each subscale in our study is 4 to 8. Lower scores are more negative (dysfunctional) and higher scores more positive (functional). There were no statistically significant differences between children in any of the four schools across these dimensions of family functioning.

A1.5.3 Child–parent communication and child involvement (*See Table 3*)

These items are similar to those developed by us for other studies (for example, Butler and others 2003). For the communication items (1–6) children selected the most appropriate response from: 'not at all', 'sometimes' and 'always'. For the

Table 3: Child–parent communication and child involvement

Items	Full study sample 48 children	Post-industrial urban school 12 children	New town urban school 12 children	Rural school 12 children	City school 12 children
1. Mother talks to child					
Not at all	–	–	–	–	–
Sometimes	32, 66.7%	7, 58.3%	7, 58.3%	10, 83.3%	8, 66.7%
Always	16, 33.3%	5, 41.7%	5, 41.7%	2, 16.7%	4, 33.3%
2. Father talks to child					
Not at all	6, 12.5%	1, 8.3%	2, 16.7%	2, 16.7%	1, 8.3%
Sometimes	29, 60.4%	6, 50.0%	9, 75.0%	5, 41.7%	9, 75.0%
Always	13, 27.1%	5, 41.7%	1, 8.3%	5, 41.7%	2, 16.7%
3. Mother and child agree					
Not at all	2, 4.2%	–	–	1, 8.3%	1, 8.3%
Sometimes	31, 64.6%	7, 58.3%	6, 50.0%	11, 91.7%	7, 58.3%
Always	15, 31.3%	5, 41.7%	6, 50.0%	–	4, 33.3%
4. Father and child agree					
Not at all	2, 4.2%	2, 16.7%	–	–	–
Sometimes	36, 75.0%	5, 41.7%	8, 66.7%	12, 100.0%	11, 91.7%
Always	10, 20.8%	5, 41.7%	4, 33.3%	–	1, 8.3%
5. Mother knows child's feeling					
Not at all	4, 8.3%	1, 8.3%	1, 8.3%	1, 8.3%	1, 8.3%
Sometimes	19, 39.6%	5, 41.7%	3, 25.0%	7, 58.3%	4, 33.3%
Always	25, 52.1%	6, 50.0%	8, 66.7%	4, 33.3%	7, 58.3%
6. Father knows child's feeling					
Not at all	8, 16.7%	–	2, 16.7%	3, 25.0%	3, 25.0%
Sometimes	25, 52.1%	8, 66.7%	6, 50.0%	6, 50.0%	5, 41.7%
Always	15, 31.3%	4, 33.3%	4, 33.3%	3, 25.0%	4, 33.3%

Table 3: Child–parent communication and child involvement (cont'd)

Items	Full study sample 48 children	Post-industrial urban school 12 children	New town urban school 12 children	Rural school 12 children	City school 12 children
7. How involved child feels					
Not at all	6, 12.5%	3, 25.0%	1, 8.3%	–	2, 16.7%
Some	24, 50.0%	4, 33.3%	5, 41.7%	9, 75.0%	6, 50.0%
Very much	18, 37.5%	5, 41.7%	6, 50.0%	3, 25.0%	4, 33.3%
8. How involved child wants to be					
Not at all	3, 6.3%	1, 8.3%	1, 8.3%	1, 8.3%	–
Some	14, 29.2%	1, 8.3%	2, 16.7%	5, 41.7%	6, 50.0%
Very much	31, 64.6%	10, 83.3%	9, 75.0%	6, 50.0%	6, 50.0%

involvement items (7–8) the choice of responses was: 'not at all', 'some' and 'very much'. The items were:

1. How often does your mum talk to you about things that happen in your family?
2. How often does your dad talk to you about things that happen in your family?
3. Do you usually agree with your mum about things that happen in your family?
4. Do you usually agree with your dad about things that happen in your family?
5. Do you think your mum usually knows what you think and feel about things that happen in your family?
6. Do you think your dad usually knows what you think and feel about things that happen in your family?
7. How involved do you feel in family issues?
8. How involved do you want to be in family issues?

There were no statistically significant differences between children in any of the four schools on these items.

A1.6 Phase 2 Activity Book data analysis and comment on study sample

It was our intention to draw a cross-sectional sample of 'normal' children (aged eight to 11) in order to examine routine, everyday decision making in families with pre-adolescent children. To aid us in this we drew our sample from 'ordinary' primary schools. That there were no significant differences between children in the four Phase 2 schools across the variables assessed indicates a degree of homogeneity across the schools. Where population norms were available (see Harter 1985), the children were within the given norms. Together these findings suggest that our sample was indeed 'ordinary' and 'normal'. As the tables indicate, however, there was variation among children themselves across the variables assessed. This, in turn, suggests we succeeded also in our other sampling objective, namely of securing a cross section of children to take part in the study.

A1.6 Phase 2 Activity Book data analysis and comment on study sample